PROPHETIC MYSTERIES
REVEALED

By LEHMAN STRAUSS

The First Person
The Second Person
The Third Person

Prophetic Mysteries Revealed
The Prophecies of Daniel
Devotional Studies in Galatians
        and Ephesians
Philippians
James Your Brother
The Epistles of John
The Book of the Revelation

Certainties for Today
The Eleven Commandments
We Live Forever

Demons, Yes—but Thank God
        for Good Angels

The Prophetic Significance
of the Parables of Matthew 13 and
the Letters of Revelation 2—3

PROPHETIC
MYSTERIES
REVEALED

BY

LEHMAN STRAUSS

LOIZEAUX BROTHERS
Neptune, New Jersey

FIRST EDITION, JULY 1980
SECOND PRINTING, NOVEMBER 1980

Library of Congress Cataloging in Publication Data

Strauss, Lehman, 1911–
  Prophetic mysteries revealed.

  Bibliography: pp. 243-245.
  Includes index.
  1. Jesus Christ—Parables. 2. Seven churches.
3. Bible. N.T. Matthew XIII—Prophecies.
4. Bible. N.T. Revelation II—III—Prophecies.
I. Title.
BT375.2.S75   226' .806   80-17540
ISBN 0-87213-832-1

Printed in the United States of America

To Deborah Marie

our sixth grandchild and only granddaughter
this volume is affectionately dedicated

CONTENTS

PREFACE

More than sixteen years have passed since my book on *The Revelation* was first published. During the months of study and writing the exposition on chapters 2 and 3, my mind went repeatedly to Matthew 13. I saw a peculiar and particular similarity in these three chapters in the Bible. Further study and research since 1963 have strengthened my first observations, hence this book.

There is nothing in these pages which has not been said by others. No claim to originality is made here. While it is impossible to acknowledge all the sources of the many helps received, the brief bibliography at the end of this volume should just about cover them.

However, one important addition to those books of other writers deserves special mention. In October 1968, while I was ministering in the Spring Hill Baptist Church in Charleston, West Virginia, Pastor William J. Wilson passed on to me a handwritten manuscript from the pen of the late Arthur W. Pink in 1912. That was exactly what I needed to encourage the writing of this book.

If only a small measure of the blessing received in preparing this manuscript is passed on to the reader, and our Lord Jesus Christ is glorified, the effort put forth in the writing of it will be well worth the time and energy spent.

LEHMAN STRAUSS

California, 1980

INTRODUCTION

In this study it is not our intention to give anything in the nature of a verse-by-verse exposition of Matthew 13 and Revelation 2 and 3. Those who wish to obtain a more comprehensive account of these three chapters can secure commentaries written by competent scholars. Our purpose here is to show the correspondence between these two portions of Scripture.

During the past one hundred years some of our ablest expositors and most efficient students of Scripture have given considerable attention to these three chapters in the New Testament. Some of these men not only differ in their viewpoints but flatly contradict each other in their interpretations. This has given some ground for the critics of the Bible to attack its authority, authenticity, and accuracy.

We Christians should not be surprised at these variations, but keep in mind the fact that the depraved nature we inherited from Adam blinds our judgment so that we are not always able to discern clearly the very truths which God caused to be written. It is to meet this need that God sent the Holy Spirit. Jesus said of the Holy Spirit that when He comes, "He shall teach you all things" (John 14:26), and "guide you into all truth" (John 16:13).

Personally, I must candidly acknowledge the difficulty

11

which I sometimes experience in approaching Scripture with an open mind, unbiased by the teaching I received in earlier days. For this reason I have prayerfully sought the help and guidance of the Holy Spirit in attempting to show the relation of these two portions of Scripture to each other. We all need to be delivered from interpreting Scripture to suit our fancy.

A fundamental principle of Biblical exegesis is laid down for us in 1 Corinthians 2:13 in the expression, *"comparing spiritual things with spiritual."* Any failure to observe this law can result in erroneous teaching. It is only as one part of Scripture is brought to bear upon another that we are enabled to grasp the Holy Spirit's meaning. It is something like fitting the pieces of a puzzle together so as to see the complete picture.

For example, 2 Thessalonians 2 throws light upon Revelation 13. Daniel 9 and 11 are the key to an understanding of Matthew 24. And so, Revelation 2—3 is an enlargement of Matthew 13, there being a remarkable unity in these three chapters. As the student examines them side by side, he sees a complete prophetic panorama of the history of Christendom from the time of its inception to the return of our Lord Jesus Christ. The same subject is developed in both portions of Scripture. Jesus referred to both as a "mystery" (Matthew 13:11; Revelation 1:20).

In some respects the Bible is like the human body. Though composed of many different members it is a unit. Just as each member has a separate function and is necessary for the completion and perfection of the whole body, so each book in the Bible plays a separate part, contributing its own being and message to complete the total scheme of divine revelation. The different parts of the Bible were written by many and varied men, yet all of it was designed, arranged, and supervised by the Holy Spirit. He has fitted each section in its appointed place and given to us a production which in variety and value is unique in the whole realm of literature.

It is because these three chapters (Matthew 13 and Revelation 2 and 3) have been so much neglected that many nominal Christians know so little about the characteristics and trends of this present age. The various books of the Bible contain, in some chapters, the key which unlocks the door of its contents, revealing important themes and subjects. The chapters to be examined in this series of studies are peculiarly precious and have a value all their own in their presentation of a course of events to take place between the two advents of Christ.

So important is the subject before us that we must approach it with sincere and humble hearts, praying that the Holy Spirit will illuminate the sacred page. We need to be receptive to His teaching that we may learn, work, and profit from ''what the Spirit saith unto the churches.''

PART ONE

THE   PARABLES   IN   MATTHEW 13

1

THE PRELIMINARY PREPARATION

The Promise of the Kingdom
The Presentation of the Kingdom
The Plot Against the King
The Postponement of the Kingdom
The Perplexity Over the Postponement

The Gospel according to Matthew is the gateway to all of the New Testament. Its position in the order and arrangement of the twenty-seven books in the New Testament is undoubtedly the work of the Holy Spirit. Understand this first book and you are on the way to an understanding of the twenty-six books that follow. Failure to understand the Gospel according to Matthew can lead to confusion for the student of the Bible.

Matthew's record is both Jewish and dispensational. Its main theme is *the King and His kingdom*. Matthew, led by the Holy Spirit, presents Jesus Christ as Israel's promised Messiah-King, of whom the Old Testament prophets wrote.

The Promise of the Kingdom

Anyone reading the Old Testament will see that human writers, inspired by the Holy Spirit, depicted the universal kingdom of God. In both His covenants and prophecies

17

the Lord repeatedly promised the establishment of His kingdom. Though our world is deteriorating politically, economically, morally, educationally, and religiously, God has a throne, and He is active on His throne. God has a kingdom. He always had a kingdom and always will. It embraces the entire universe.

First, the kingdom of God is described in Scripture as being *unlimited* and *unrestricted* in its scope. The Psalmist wrote, "The LORD hath prepared His throne in the heavens; and His kingdom ruleth over all" (Psalm 103:19). This passage speaks of God's sovereign rule over all His vast creation. Nebuchadnezzar was given to see the universal rule of God when he testified, "I blessed the most High, and I praised and honoured Him that liveth for ever, whose dominion is an everlasting dominion, and His kingdom is from generation to generation: And all the inhabitants of the earth are reputed as nothing: and He doeth according to His will in the army of heaven, and among the inhabitants of the earth: and none can stay His hand, or say unto Him, what doest Thou?" (Daniel 4:34-35) This is the eternal and absolute rule of God over His universe and all His creatures.

Secondly, the Bible speaks also of that aspect of God's kingdom that is *limited* and *restricted* both as to scope and time. It is God's kingdom on earth, localized and temporal. This earthly kingdom was included in the Abrahamic Covenant (Genesis 12:1-3; 13:14-17; 15:1-18; 17:1-19; 26:3-5; 28:13-15), which covenant God confirmed with Isaac and Jacob. The Davidic Covenant likewise included an earthly kingdom. In it God gave to David and his seed an unconditional promise of a king and a kingdom (2 Samuel 7). Moreover, it was clear to the Old Testament prophets that the throne would be on earth in Jerusalem (Isaiah 2:3; Micah 4:2). The Old Testament Scriptures left no doubt in the minds of the Jewish people that Israel as a nation would one day have a righteous King to rule over them (Jeremiah 23:5-6), and that His kingdom would be one of earthwide peace (Isaiah 2:3-4; Micah 4:1-4).

The promise of the kingdom could not be disassociated from the presence of the King. A kingdom demands a king. This was a fact well known which gave to Israel the confident expectation of their Messiah's coming. They were looking for their Conqueror who would throw off the Roman yoke and set up the glorious Davidic-Messianic kingdom.

One night Nebuchadnezzar had a dream. It was so terrifying that it awakened him. When he awoke he completely forgot what he had dreamed. Daniel was summoned, to whom God revealed the king's dream and its interpretation. Daniel told the king that in his dream he saw an image of a man, tall and great. Its head was made of gold, the breast and arms of silver, the belly and thighs of brass, legs of iron, and feet part of iron and part of clay. The four metals of which the image was made represented four Gentile empires, each with a representative head. The first empire was Babylon, the head of gold representing Nebuchadnezzar. Babylon would be succeeded by the Medo-Persian Empire, which in turn would be followed by the kingdoms of Greece and Rome, in that order (Daniel 2).

The dream contained much more. Daniel told

Nebuchadnezzar that in the dream he saw a stone strike the image upon its feet, crashing it to the ground and grinding it to powder. The wind carried the dust away so that the residue disappeared completely. Then the stone that destroyed the image increased in size until it filled the whole earth (Daniel 2:35).

The interpretation was clear and unmistakable. "And in the days of these kings shall the God of heaven set up a kingdom, which shall never be destroyed: and the kingdom shall not be left to other people, but it shall break in pieces and consume all these kingdoms, and it shall stand for ever" (Daniel 2:44). When God places His King upon His holy hill in Zion (Psalm 2:6), all earthly kingdoms will be done away. There is no place on earth for God's kingdom and the kingdoms of this world. They will be destroyed completely when the King of kings takes over the rule on earth. In that day "the government shall be upon His shoulder" (Isaiah 9:6).

That stone in Nebuchadnezzar's dream is Jesus Christ. He is the Chief Corner Stone, the Father's elect and precious One, the Stone which the builders rejected (1 Peter 2:6-8). He is the promised King. The very title "Christ" means the *Anointed*, suggesting kingship. He is the predicted ruler in Genesis 49:10; David's righteous Branch, who shall reign as King in Jeremiah 23:5, the One whose right it is to wear the diadem in Ezekiel 21:26-27; He that is to be ruler in Israel in Micah 5:2; and the King who shall rule over all the earth in Zechariah 9:9 and 14:9.

When Nathanael hailed Christ as the "King of Israel" (John 1:49), he gave evidence of having some knowledge of the prophetic Scriptures in the Old Testament. The

Messiah had been promised, therefore the Jewish people should have been expecting Him.

The Presentation of the Kingdom

After the birth of Jesus Christ the request of the wise men from the east was, "Where is He that is born *King* of the Jews?" (Matthew 2:2) The earliest preaching of John the Baptist had as its major message, "Repent ye: for the *kingdom* of heaven is at hand" (3:2). Following our Lord's baptism He preached the same message (4:17). Matthew said that Jesus went about Galilee "preaching the gospel of the *kingdom*" (4:23; 9:35). Then when our Lord sent forth His twelve disciples He told them, "And as ye go, preach, saying, The *kingdom* of heaven is at hand" (10:7). The message was the same whether it was preached by John, Jesus, or His disciples: "The *kingdom* of heaven is at hand." Not that the kingdom had come, but rather that the King was present to offer His kingdom.

But the Jewish leaders rejected Christ as their promised Messiah even though they were well acquainted with the Messianic prophecies which told that David's greater Son would reign (2 Samuel 7). They knew further that the throne was to be on earth in Jerusalem, not in Heaven (Isaiah 2:3; Micah 4:2). Those who tell us that John the Baptist was merely appealing to individuals for personal repentance are in error. They are proved to be wrong in the light of the angel Gabriel's announcement to Mary, "And, behold, thou shalt conceive in thy womb, and bring forth a son, and shalt call His name JESUS. He shall be great, and shall be called the Son of the Highest: and the Lord God shall give unto Him the throne of His father David: And He shall reign over the house of Jacob for ever; and of His kingdom there shall be no end" (Luke 1:31-33). Those Jews who rejected Christ as their Messiah could not plead ignorance.

In the first eleven chapters Matthew presents our Lord's rightful claim to the throne of David. His *genealogical* right through His ancestor David is stated in chapters 1 and 2. His *personal* claim to be King follows with the approbation and approval announced by the Father (3:17). His *moral* right to the kingship He proved in His triumph over the temptations of Satan recorded in chapter 4. The precepts and principles of the kingdom Christ taught with authority in the Sermon on the Mount (chapters 5—7). He demonstrated His right to be King by His power and authority over defilement (8:1-4), distance (8:28-34), death (9:18-26), and dumbness (9:32-33). And all the while He continued in "the cities and villages, teaching in their synagogues, and preaching the gospel of the *kingdom*" (9:35).

In a brief period of time our Lord demonstrated in every way possible His right to be King. In His teaching, in His moral behavior, and in His supernatural and miraculous deeds, He showed to all what conditions will be like when He rules and reigns on the earth. He was not the typical politician making promises to the people in order to win an election. Christ was no political Messiah. He came to save men from sin and sinning. The nature of His kingdom is spiritual. In chapters 5—7 He made His inaugural address and declared the manifesto of the kingdom, and then He followed that up with demonstrative proof that He had both the power and authority to give to the people a utopia. He authenticated His Messianic claims in a most convincing fashion. He was the one and only Person with the qualifications to fill the office of King of Israel. Everything connected with the coming of the King was of a convincing character. He was truly "Emmanuel ... God with us" (Matthew 1:23; cf., Isaiah 7:14).

The Plot Against the King

In Matthew 12 a storm of rejection arose against our Lord through the action of Israel's responsible leaders. In their first attack against Him they accused Him of breaking the Mosaic Law, the fourth commandment in particular, "Remember the sabbath day, to keep it holy" (Exodus 20:8-11). Matthew relates that Jesus permitted His disciples to gather corn on the Sabbath (12:1-9), and then He healed the man with a withered hand (12:10-13). At this point in his narrative Matthew says, "Then the Pharisees went out, and held a council against Him, how they might destroy Him" (12:14). It was an open and defiant rejection of the King.

But the most vicious attack by which the Jewish leaders rejected Jesus was when they accused Him of being in league with Satan. One possessed with a demon, blind and dumb, was brought to our Lord, and He healed him. "And all the people were amazed, and said, Is not this the son of David?" (12:22-23) The favorable response of the people infuriated the Pharisees to malignant hatred. In their hostility they charged our Lord with performing miracles by the power of Satan. This was no mere unbelief on their part, but a deliberate and vicious perversion of the truth, a flagrant apostasy for which there was no forgiveness (12:24-32). Individual Jews could be saved through faith in Christ's forthcoming death and resurrection, but the nation of Israel, through her official leaders, was now committed to the rejection of her King. It was a sad day for both Israel and her Messiah. In rejecting the King they rejected the kingdom. They were not for Him, therefore, they were against Him (12:30).

At this point in our study we can profit from a look into another critical period in Israel's history. It was during the time of the Judges. The Scripture says, "In those days there was *no king* in Israel, but every man did that which was right in his own eyes" (Judges 17:6; 18:1; 19:1; 21:25). There was *"no king in Israel,"* a characteristic phrase occurring four times; and *"every man did that which was right in his own eyes,"* a phrase appearing twice, depicts the state of the people. Every man did his own thing with utter disregard for authority. Authority was not with God, nor with a God-appointed leader, but with man himself. The history of man trying to rule himself is a history of spiritual and moral declension, of departure from God. The ideal form of government is not *democracy*, which is the rule of man, but *theocracy* which is the rule of God. The period of the Judges was a time of national disaster for Israel. There was no king. They were not in subjection to the rule of God.

History is repeating itself. The King of kings has been rejected by the world. Our Lord said in another parable, "His citizens hated Him, and sent a message after Him, saying, We will not have this man to reign over us" (Luke 19:14). The reason why Christ spoke this parable is given by Luke: "because He was nigh to Jerusalem, and because they thought that the *kingdom* of God should immediately appear" (Luke 19:11). Our Lord was approaching the city of Jerusalem, the city of the King, the place from which He would rule over His kingdom. It was not strange that many persons, including the disciples, had a strong feeling—that is, it seemed to them—that something of great magnitude was about to happen. Both Jesus and John had preached that the kingdom of God was at hand. Many persons expected that in this visit to Jerusalem Christ would fulfill that prophetic expectation of the Jewish nation, break the yoke of Roman bondage, declare His authority, and take over the reins of government. But they were mistaken. Luke states clearly that it was because of their faulty reasoning that our Lord spoke this parable.

The Postponement of the Kingdom

The first lesson to be learned from this parable of the pounds is that the rejection of the King necessitated the postponement of the establishing of His kingdom. Now don't think for one second that Christ laid aside His regal authority. He was and is the King even now. It was the full manifestation of His power and authority with the accompanying blessing that was postponed. At this very moment He is "the blessed and only Potentate, the King of kings, and Lord of lords" (1 Timothy 6:15).

After His death and resurrection He "went into a far

country to receive for Himself a kingdom, and to return" (Luke 19:12). Upon His arrival into the far country (Heaven), "God also hath highly exalted Him, and given Him a name which is above every name: That at the name of Jesus every knee should bow, of things in heaven, and things in earth, and things under the earth; And that every tongue should confess that Jesus Christ is Lord, to the glory of God the Father" (Philippians 2:9-11). Here the apostle is saying that Christ is crowned now. His coronation took place "when He ascended up on high" (Ephesians 4:8), and "sat down on the right hand of the Majesty on high" (Hebrews 1:3). He is reigning now.

The postponement of the kingdom is the deferring of the visible and physical kingdom on earth with the King present. This does not mean that the promises God made to Israel in the Old Testament have been canceled. The kingdom will be established but not until Israel is ready to accept Christ as her Messiah. Keep in mind the fact that when Christ offered the kingdom to Israel He did so in sincerity, but remember also that He offered it conditionally. In every announcement stating that the kingdom was "at hand," there was the accompanying command to *repent*. Inasmuch as the kingdom was national the repentance must of necessity be national. All must repent and receive the Messiah, including the Pharisees, priests, rabbis, and the common people. Early in our Lord's ministry He made it clear that a spiritual rebirth was a condition for entering His kingdom. He said, "Verily, verily, I say unto thee, Except a man be born again, he cannot see the *kingdom* of God" (John 3:3). This message from Christ to the Pharisee Nicodemus contained the same condition demanded of every person, Jew and Gentile. When Israel rejected the King she rejected the kingdom.

The kingdom condition was laid down by Christ explicitly when He said, "For I say unto you, That except your righteousness shall exceed the righteousness of the scribes and Pharisees, ye shall in no case enter into the *kingdom* of heaven" (Matthew 5:20). There is no place in God's kingdom for unrighteous persons. The "righteousness" of the scribes and Pharisees was a human self-righteousness of which the Bible says, "All our righteousnesses are as filthy rags" (Isaiah 64:6). Speaking of Israel, Paul said, "For they being ignorant of God's righteousness, and going about to establish their own righteousness, have not submitted themselves unto the righteousness of God" (Romans 10:3). He who rejects the righteous King is unfit for His kingdom. Having no righteousness of our own we must "be made the righteousness of God in Him" (2 Corinthians 5:21). When we receive Him we receive His righteousness (1 Corinthians 1:30). When Israel rejected the King the kingdom was deferred.

Have you ever noticed those "exceptions" of Jesus? Each one contains a condition for entering the kingdom. "*Except* a man be born again, he cannot see the *kingdom* of God" (John 3:3). "*Except* your righteousness shall exceed the righteousness of the scribes and Pharisees, ye shall in no case enter into the *kingdom* of heaven" (Matthew 5:20). "*Except* ye be converted, and become as little children, ye shall not enter into the *kingdom* of heaven" (Matthew 18:3). The first exception in John 3:5

requires *regeneration*. The second exception in Matthew 5:20 demands *righteousness*. The third exception in Matthew 18:3 calls for *renunciation*, that is, the renouncing of self. The Jewish leaders had rejected all three of our Lord's "exceptions," and because of this the kingdom was deferred. God requires kingdom righteousness of the subjects of His kingdom, but such righteousness can be experienced only in that person who permits the King to reign in his life.

The Perplexity Over the Postponement

There is disagreement and even dispute as to whether or not the kingdom as predicted in the Old Testament and offered by our Lord was actually postponed. The problem is a real one and it lingers as a debatable issue.

One author wrote: "The kingdom Jesus offered was not that theocratic kingdom of which the Old Testament speaks. If it was, then it follows that if the people had accepted Christ and His offer, the literal earthly manifestation of the kingdom would have been realized at once. But then, the necessity for the work of redemption through Christ's death on the cross would thereupon never have arisen. The cross would then have been a conditional factor in the mind of God. Christ would not have died if Israel would have accepted the proffered kingdom; there would be no redemption for us and we would all be lost."

To some persons the above statement seems logical and is therefore convincing. But the Biblical records show otherwise. Luke recorded an interesting discussion between our Lord and the Pharisees which bears heavily in favor of the offer of the kingdom being a legitimate one. "And when He was demanded of the Pharisees, when the kingdom of God should come, He answered them and said, The kingdom of God cometh not with observation" (Luke 17:20). The word "observation" means literally, "with outward show, fanfare, pomp, and ceremony."

Jesus continued, "Neither shall they say, Lo here! or, lo there! for, behold, the kingdom of God is within you" (Luke 17:21). By this statement He meant that the kingdom was then *in their midst, it was among them* because He, the King, was at that time presenting Himself to them. And then, turning to His disciples He added, "But first must He suffer many things, and be rejected of this generation" (Luke 17:25). Now they could not reject something if it had not been offered to them. Christ was standing in their midst and telling them that the kingdom was then in their midst. But they rejected Him. A legitimate rejection precludes a legitimate offer.

But let me assure you that Israel's rejection of Christ and His bona fide offer of the kingdom did not take God by surprise. Though the Jews, by their own free will, made the tragic choice to reject their Messiah, God's sovereign plan and purpose were carried out in every detail. Look again at those words of our Lord, "But *first* must He suffer many things, and be rejected of this generation." Before the kingdom could be set up, His suffering and rejection must come *first*. This was the order in which God planned these events. After our Lord's resurrection He said to the two travelers enroute to Emmaus, "O fools, and slow of heart to believe all that the prophets have spoken: Ought not Christ to have suffered these things, and to enter into

His glory?'' (Luke 24:25-26) He reminded them that His sufferings and rejection had to precede His glorious reign.

The crucifixion and death of Christ was a frustrating surprise to His disciples, but it was ''by the determinate counsel and foreknowledge of God'' (Acts 2:23). Jesus Himself said, ''Even as the Son of man came not to be ministered unto, but to minister, and to give His life a ransom for many'' (Matthew 20:28). Christ came to die. One of the purposes of His Incarnation was, ''that through death He might destroy him that had the power of death, that is, the devil'' (Hebrews 2:14); ''that He by the grace of God should taste death for *every man*'' (Hebrews 2:9).

Someone might ask, ''How then can we reconcile divine sovereignty and human responsibility?'' Both truths are taught in the Bible; they are friends and do not need to be reconciled. God is sovereign and elects sinners to salvation, but not all sinners will be saved. Christ died for all, but many will be lost (see John 1:29; 11:51-53; Romans 2:4; 1 Timothy 2:4; 2 Peter 3:9; 1 John 2:2). I have yet to meet the theologian or Bible teacher, personally or through his writings, who could explain fully and with perfect clarity this great mystery. God loves, and provides salvation for, the whole world of mankind (John 3:16), and yet, ''He that believeth not the Son shall not see life; but the wrath of God abideth on him'' (John 3:36). God's offer to sinners to be saved is a genuine and bona fide offer, and yet He knows that many to whom the offer is made will reject it. His foreknowledge of what man will do does not determine man's decision. Those who reject Christ are responsible for their action.

Why would God make such an offer knowing that some

to whom the offer is presented would refuse it? Paul answers this question, in part at least, in his Epistle to the Romans where he says, "so that they are without excuse" (Romans 1:20). The marginal reading has it, "so that they may be without excuse." As we stated earlier in this study, our Lord gave every evidence that He was Israel's Messiah. Their rejection of Him placed them in the position of responsibility. Seven hundred years before Christ came, God told the Prophet Isaiah to preach to the nation, and yet He told Isaiah beforehand that the people would not believe the message but reject it (Isaiah 6:9-10). The prophet preached God's message in sincerity, knowing the hearers would not heed it. Their refusal to heed the message made them responsible. God's foreknowledge of the people's rejection of His message did not exonerate them.

But there was another reason why God acted as He did in dealing with Israel. And this brings us to the heart of our study. God never intended to offer salvation to only one nation and arbitrarily consign the rest of the world to eternal judgment. When Christ came to earth it was for the purpose of dying for the whole human race, "that He by the grace of God should taste death for every man" (Hebrews 2:9). It is in the parables in Matthew 13 that we have the total picture of God's plan for all mankind.

2

THE PURPOSE OF THE PARABLES

And the disciples came, and said unto Him, Why speakest Thou unto them in parables? He answered and said unto them, Because it is given unto you to know the mysteries of the kingdom of heaven, but to them it is not given. For whosoever hath, to him shall be given, and he shall have more abundance: but whosoever hath not, from him shall be taken away even that he hath. Therefore speak I to them in parables: because they seeing see not; and hearing they hear not, neither do they understand. And in them is fulfilled the prophecy of Esaias, which saith, By hearing ye shall hear, and shall not understand; and seeing ye shall see, and shall not perceive: For this people's heart is waxed gross, and their ears are dull of hearing, and their eyes they have closed; lest at any time they should see with their eyes, and hear with their ears, and should understand with their heart, and should be converted, and I should heal them. But blessed are your eyes, for they see; and your ears, for they hear. For verily I say unto you, That many prophets and righteous men have desired to see those things which ye see, and have not seen them; and to hear those things which ye hear, and have not heard them (Matthew 13:10-17).

Before we study the parables in Matthew 13, there is an interesting and informative interlude in verses 10-16. It is in the form of a question asked by the disciples and our Lord's answer. The question and its answer is a seeming departure from the chronological order of events, ap-

pearing between the giving of the first parable and
Christ's interpretation of it.

We are not told precisely what it was that prompted the
disciples to ask their question. Now take note of the fact
that they did not ask Jesus why He spoke in parables, but
why He spoke to *them* (the multitudes who gathered to
hear Him). That word *them* is the key to the question. The
parabolic form of teaching was not a novelty, it was not a
brand-new method of teaching. But never before had
Jesus addressed the *multitudes* in this way. The disciples
had never heard our Lord talk this way to the crowds, and
they could not understand it.

They must have heard His answer with pleasure and
delight when He said, "Because it is given unto *you* to
know the mysteries of the kingdom of heaven, but to
them it is not given" (verse 11). Don't overlook that word
"given." It suggests the idea of pure grace. Divine
revelation is always a matter of grace on God's part.

But along with divine sovereignty there is also the
matter of human responsibility, and this tells us why the
disciples were given the mysteries and the multitudes were
not. "For whosoever hath, to him shall be given, and he
shall have more abundance: but whosoever hath not, from
him shall be taken away even that he hath" (verse 12).
Any misinterpretation of these words of Christ will lead to
misunderstanding, therefore let us examine them carefully.

Jesus had just said, "It is given unto *you* to know ... but
to *them* it is not given"! To the one group the parable
revealed truth; to the other it *concealed* it. This was not an
arbitrary act on God's part. The parables were not spoken

deliberately to hinder the crowds from understanding our Lord's teaching. This I strongly deny to be so. The crowd that was not part of the "in" group could blame nobody but themselves.

In our Lord's words in verse 12 you will find a basic, fundamental principle of life. It is simply this: *what we do not use we lose*. Suppose your arm were fastened securely in a sling for a long period of time so that you did not use one muscle in that arm. You would discover that the arm would begin to atrophy and weaken. If you didn't use the arm you would lose the ability to use it.

In the parable of the sower, Jesus is speaking about how people hear the Word of God. He said, "Who hath ears to hear, let him hear" (verse 9). Luke added the words, "Take heed therefore how ye hear" (Luke 8:18). The disciples had heard Christ's words and responded to them, therefore to them He would give more truth. The multitudes had heard His words and rejected them. They had eyes to see, ears to hear, and hearts to understand, but they refused to see, hear, and understand. The truth they refused is now lost to them. They lacked what the disciples possessed, namely, divine truth. Their ignorance was willful ignorance. They *did not* understand because they *would not* understand. Theirs was a deliberate rejection of the truth. They didn't have it because they didn't want it, therefore, "whosoever hath not, from him shall be taken away even that he hath" (Matthew 13:12). When Jesus called Simon, Andrew, James, and John, "they immediately ... followed Him" (Matthew 4:18-22). They heard Christ speak and acted upon His Word, so to them and to the others who obeyed the truth was given to know the secrets; but from those who rejected the truth they were withheld.

During my years in the pastorate I have watched both classes, those who heard the truth and obeyed it and others who heard the same truth but refused to act upon it. I have witnessed spiritual growth in the lives of many, and in every instance they were diligent students of the Bible, obeying its precepts and advancing to Christian maturity. And so God continued to give them more truth.

Our Lord continues answering the disciples' question by quoting the Prophet Isaiah:

> And in them is fulfilled the prophecy of Esaias, which saith, By hearing ye shall hear, and shall not understand; and seeing ye shall see, and shall not perceive: For this people's heart is waxed gross, and their ears are dull of hearing, and their eyes they have closed; lest at any time they should see with their eyes, and hear with their ears, and should understand with their heart, and should be converted, and I should heal them (Matthew 13:14-15).

Now please note that it was not God who hardened their hearts, stopped their ears, and closed their eyes to the truth. They did it themselves, deliberately, voluntarily, and knowingly. They knew what God's plan was for them, but they did not want it, choosing rather their own folly and fleshly desires. Isaiah said the people would close their own eyes lest they should see, and turn a deaf ear on the truth lest they should hear. And that is why Jesus said, "Who hath ears to hear, let him hear" (verse 9). Any person who anesthetizes his heart, muffles his ears, and shuts his eyes to the Word of God, God will punish by allowing him to have his way.

But the very opposite is true of all who receive Christ and His Word. Our Lord says to all such, ''Blessed are your eyes, for they see: And your ears, for they hear'' (verse 16). God reveals truth to those who continue to obey it. Obedience to the truth creates the capacity for more truth. The difference in our Lord's method of teaching in parables was a result of a difference in relationship with Him. The disciples who received Him would now know the mysteries of the kingdom. To the multitudes who had hardened their hearts and did not want to know, the parabolic method applied.

Now this does not mean that the secrets of the kingdom were not discoverable to any among the multitude. Any person hearing those parables, and repenting of their hardness of heart and seeking their true meaning, would know the truth Jesus taught. The parables are an appeal to the heart of man and an open door to the truth.

''Hear ye therefore the parable of the sower'' (verse 18). Now we can see that the disciples' question and our Lord's reply are not chronologically out of place. ''Hear ye *therefore*....'' If there was no hope for any of them, Jesus would not have appealed to them to pay close attention to His interpretation of that first parable. In substance He is saying to them, ''Until now you have hardened your heart, closed your eyes, and muffled your ears, *therefore*, pay close attention to this parable.''

The giving of these parables must be regarded as a divine judgment upon the nation of Israel because ''*they have closed*'' their own eyes to the truth. I will not argue as to whether the parables were given to *produce* blindness, or as a *result* of blindness. One point is decisive, namely, the context of Isaiah 6:9-10 and its quotation in the New Testament cannot change the judicial nature of our Lord's words. The blindness of the multitude to the mysteries of the kingdom is represented as judicial, a punishment inflicted by God upon a people who deliberately closed their eyes to divine truth (Matthew 13:15). It is in keeping with the nature of God to judge men for their willful unbelief.

We may conclude, therefore, that we have in these parables the principle of double purpose, both beneficial and retributive. This principle applies to all persons in every dispensation. It is dangerous for any of us to muffle our ears and shut our eyes to God's truth.

In this series of parables our Lord was about to reveal that which had been hitherto unrevealed. He will now bring to light that which had been hidden and secret. The time has now come for the King to make known to His subjects those events to follow His first appearing and continue until His second coming. The events He is about to reveal will occur during this present age. Here then is an outline of certain events depicting the course of this present age from the rejection of the Messiah by Israel until His reception by Israel at His second coming to the earth. The clear knowledge of those events requires the proper interpretation of the parables recorded in Matthew 13.

Matthew 13 is a very important chapter in the Bible and a crucial chapter in Matthew's record. It contains one of three kingdom discourses spoken by our Lord. All three are related to Christ and His kingdom: the principles of the kingdom (chapters 5—7); the parables of the kingdom (chapter 13); the prophecies of the King (chapters 24—25).

The parables of the kingdom will engage our thoughts and meditations in the following pages. Matthew 13 contains seven parables spoken by Jesus (some writers see eight parables in this chapter). The purpose of this particular series of parables is to teach what our Lord called "the *mysteries* of the kingdom of heaven" (13:11).

The word "mystery" is sometimes misunderstood. It has been brought over to us from the Greek word *musterion*. It does not suggest the idea of mysteriousness, but rather a truth which heretofore has been hidden but is now revealed. Many lodges are secret societies, having secrets which nonmembers do not know. But once the neophyte is initiated into the lodge, the aura of mystery disappears because the secret is now made known. The purpose of our Lord in relating this series of parables was to reveal truth which God has seen fit to keep secret until Israel's leaders rejected Christ as their Messiah. "All these things spake Jesus unto the multitude in parables; and without a parable spake He not unto them: That it might be fulfilled which was spoken by the prophet, saying, I will open my mouth in parables; I will utter things which have been kept secret from the foundation of the world" (13:34-35).

In these seven parables our Lord revealed things which had been kept secret from the foundation of the world. The responsible leaders in Israel had rejected their King. It is now God's time to tell them that something important is about to happen. The King is going to return to Heaven, and during His absence, before He returns to earth to establish the kingdom they had rejected, the seed of God's Word must be sown in all the world. *Now*, "the field is the world" (13:38), not merely Palestine and the Jews.

The secret which the Old Testament prophets did not see was that at Messiah's first coming He would be rejected, die on the cross, rise from death and the grave, go back to Heaven, and then come to earth a second time in glory to establish His kingdom. The prophets saw the coming golden age, but they did not see the time period between Christ's two appearings, now more than nineteen hundred years. They saw both His "sufferings" and "the glory that should follow" (1 Peter 1:10-11), but the "time" between those two events was the "mystery" about which they searched diligently. The "kingdom of heaven" was no secret to Israel.

The *mystery* was the fact that there would be a long period of time, the church age, in which God would not deal with Israel as a nation but send the gospel into all the world. God, in His compassion for the entire race of mankind, purposed from eternity to redeem people from every tribe and nation. This is the great *mystery*, that God would set aside His chosen people Israel, so that He might redeem sinners from among the Gentiles as well as Jews.

The parables in Matthew 13 are a description of the kingdom of Heaven during this present age. The kingdom of Heaven in this age is not the Church. If we equate the kingdom of Heaven in Matthew 13 with the Church, we create confusion. Matthew 13 includes a longer period of time than is involved in the church age. The *kingdom in mystery* commenced with the *rejection* of the King in

Matthew 12 and will conclude with the *return* of the King
at the end of the tribulation. The *kingdom in manifestation* will follow the tribulation and continue for 1,000
years. While we must not equate the *mystery* form of the
kingdom with the church age, it does include the church
era. In these parables we have the form that the kingdom
of Heaven will take on earth during the King's absence.
The Church is never called the kingdom of Heaven.

The first appearance of the words *parable* and *mystery*
in the New Testament are here in Matthew 13 (verses
3,11). These parables relate to the secrets of the kingdom
of Heaven. They are particularly prophetical and
dispensational. They were uttered to show the varied
responses and reactions to the Word of God during the
King's absence. The teaching Christ unfolded in these
parables was new truth, held in secret by God until Jesus
taught it. The kingdom of Heaven in these parables
represents *professing Christianity*, identified frequently by
the term *Christendom*.

Some people are not aware of the fact that the Bible
contains a record of church history beyond that which
appears in the book of Acts. They have not the slightest
idea of what would take place after these events recorded
in Acts. But we are not left without divinely inspired help
on this subject. There are several significant passages of
Scripture which present a broad panoramic view of what
would follow in human history after Christ's ascension to
Heaven and the founding of His Church.

One of these passages is Matthew 13. I propose that we
examine these parables prayerfully and carefully. In them
we will see history as Jesus taught it. We will see events as

God saw them and predicted them. The world sees history only as man views it. After one has read the most accurate and best-written histories, he has only a repetition of the birth and death of world leaders, kings, queens, dictators, premiers, presidents; the rise and fall of nations and empires; the record of wars, exploitations, catastrophies, and sorrow; and the report of scientific progress. History at its best from man's viewpoint is a sordid, twisted view of things.

If you want an accurate picture of history and a prophetic preview of what to look for while our Lord is absent from the earth, these parables will tell you. What can we expect as regards the reception of God's Word? What can we look for in the way of opposition to the proclamation of the gospel? Can we expect a worldwide conversion to Christ before He comes again? Will peace come to the earth? What will Satan's method of opposition be to God's truth during this present age? What is Israel's future? These and other questions are answered clearly in the teachings of our Lord in these seven parables.

Matthew records all seven parables. Mark wrote about two of them: the parables of the sower and mustard seed (Mark 4:1-9,13-20,30-32). In Luke's record we have the parables of the sower, the mustard seed (Luke 8:5-15), and the leaven (Luke 13:20-21).

3

THE PARABLE OF THE SOWER

And He spake many things unto them in parables, saying, Behold, a sower went forth to sow; And when he sowed, some seeds fell by the way side, and the fowls came and devoured them up: Some fell upon stony places, where they had not much earth; and forthwith they sprung up, because they had no deepness of earth. And when the sun was up, they were scorched; and because they had no root, they withered away. And some fell among thorns; and the thorns sprung up, and choked them: But other fell into good ground, and brought forth fruit, some an hundredfold, some sixtyfold, some thirtyfold. Who hath ears to hear, let him hear. Hear ye therefore the parable of the sower. When any one heareth the Word of the kingdom, and understandeth it not, then cometh the wicked one, and catcheth away that which was sown in his heart. This is he which received seed by the way side. But he that received the seed into stony places, the same is he that heareth the Word, and anon with joy receiveth it; Yet hath he not root in himself, but endureth for a while: for when tribulation or persecution ariseth because of the Word, by and by he is offended. He also that received seed among the thorns is he that heareth the Word; and the care of this world, and the deceitfulness of riches, choke the Word, and he becometh unfruitful. But he that received seed into the good ground is he that heareth the Word, and understandeth it; which also beareth fruit, and bringeth forth, some an hundredfold, some sixty, some thirty (Matthew 13:3-9,18-23).

In the Old Testament God likens Himself to a *sower*

42

(Jeremiah 31:27). Likewise His children are sowers (Psalm 126:5-6). But here in the parable Jesus Himself is the sower as He introduces His program to be carried on during His absence. In His second parable in this series of seven He said, "He that soweth the good seed is the Son of man" (Matthew 13:37).

The *seed* in the parable is the Word of God, called "the *Word* of the kingdom" (Matthew 13:19). Mark said, "The sower soweth the *Word*" (Mark 4:14). Luke states plainly, "Now the parable is this: The seed is *the Word of God*" (Luke 8:11). It is the living, life-giving seed with its own inherent power to deal with sin in the human heart (Hebrews 4:12), and to bring to pass the new birth (1 Peter 1:23). It is the Word of truth that begets life in sinners (James 1:18) and saves their souls (James 1:21).

During the King's absence His followers are to go to all the world and preach the Word to every creature (Mark 16:15), even to "the uttermost part of the earth" (Acts 1:8). Here then we have the King's prophetic program for His own followers during the present dispensation. The worldwide sowing of the seed of God's Word is the divine program for the Church of Christ. We must guard against being sidetracked into becoming involved with lesser things.

The *soils* in the parable, four in number, represent four classes of hearers, each with a different response to God's Word. The outstanding feature of the parable is the attention our Lord focuses on the soils. Those soils represent the human "heart" (Matthew 13:19; Mark 4:15; Luke 8:12,15). In the four soils our Lord is predicting the various types of listeners the sowers of the Word will encounter. We learn from this what response to expect from those who hear the Word of God. Here we have the parable of listening ears and responsive hearts. This is an outstanding feature of the parable.

The Way Side. "And when he sowed, some seeds fell by the way side, and the fowls came and devoured them up.... When any one heareth the Word of the kingdom, and understandeth it not, then cometh the wicked one, and catcheth away that which was sown in his heart. This is he which received seed by the way side" (Matthew 13:4,19). In this instance the seed fell upon the common path beaten hard by the feet of those who walked that route. The surface was so hard that there was little chance of the seed penetrating it, and so it fell prey to the birds who hovered overhead ready to devour it.

This is the *unconcerned* heart, the *hard* heart. This heart, owing to its hardness, *did not take in the seed*. The King James Version says that the heart "understandeth it not." The fault did not lie in the seed, nor in the sower, but in the soil of the human heart. It was not a case of mental incapacity or lack of intellectual understanding. The seed fell on the surface, that is, it was received by the ear, but because of the hardness of the heart it never germinated. It is possible that this indifferent hearer heard the Word on a regular basis.

The *hard* and *unconcerned* heart is easy prey for Satan. The hardhearted are those "in whom the god of this world hath blinded the minds of them which believe not, lest the light of the glorious gospel of Christ, who is the image of God, should shine unto them" (2 Corinthians 4:4). When they will not understand, Jesus said, "then cometh the wicked one, and catcheth away that which was sown in his heart" (Matthew 13:19). The heart in which the Word of God is received and obeyed is never overcome by Satan. "I write unto you, young men, because ye have overcome the wicked one ... ye are strong, and *the Word of God abideth in you*, and ye have overcome the wicked one" (1 John 2:13-14). Yes, there are those who hear the Word, "but when they have heard, Satan cometh immediately, and taketh away the Word that was sown in their hearts" (Mark 4:15). Luke wrote, "Those by the way side are they that hear; then cometh the devil, and taketh away the Word out of their hearts, lest they should believe and be saved" (Luke 8:12).

The first part of this parable was true when our Lord spoke it. The hard hearts of the Jewish leaders had rejected His words, and already Satan had taken the Word out of their hearts. But our Lord was speaking prophetically of the entire period during His absence. We are sure that many who hear will not receive the Word and be saved. There will not be a universal reception of the truth, as postmillenarians teach. The parable foreshadows the end times, warning us that we are doomed to bitter disappointment if we cherish romantic expectations that through the preaching of God's Word the world will get better and better through the universal acceptance of the gospel of Christ.

The Stony Ground. "Some fell upon stony places, where they had not much earth: and forthwith they sprung up, because they had no deepness of earth: And when the sun was up, they were scorched; and because they had no root, they withered away" (Matthew 13:5-6).

Jesus then explained the heart of the stony-ground hearer. "But he that received the seed into stony places, the same is he that heareth the Word, and anon with joy receiveth it; Yet hath he not root in himself, but endureth for a while: for when tribulation or persecution ariseth because of the Word, by and by he is offended" (Matthew 13:20-21).

The stony ground was probably a strata of limestone rock with a thin covering of earth on top. The seed would germinate quickly. Mark says, "*Immediately* it sprang up" (Mark 4:5). And then, in recording our Lord's interpretation of the stony-ground hearers, he uses that word *immediately* twice more. When they have heard the Word they "immediately receive it with gladness" (Mark 4:16). But when trials or tribulation come to them, "immediately they are offended" (Mark 4:17). They responded speedily, and with equal alacrity they rejected the Word.

Many hearts are like thin shallow soil. They respond readily to any new thing. They follow new fashions, respond enthusiastically to a famous personality who is popular at the time. They are the emotional type who are swept off their feet easily. They hear the Word and with lighthearted joy respond to it, but they are shallow, having no depth. These stony-ground hearers heard the Word and showed an outward enthusiasm for it for a while.

Every person is by nature capable of responding to an appeal, especially an appeal to the emotions. There is today much of that kind of preaching that has in it an emotional appeal, but the appeal is to the flesh. It grabs the emotional hearer, and if there is any conviction it is fleshly conviction. Dr. Paul Van Gorder said, "I have never been in favor of getting a sinner up from his knees and showing him off in front of a crowd. Irreparable harm has been done to the cause of Christ by parading noted figures of the entertainment, sports, and political world across the evangelical platform before sufficient time has elapsed to indicate whether the seed of the Word of God has penetrated and really taken root." The first effect of the gospel should be not to exalt a personality, but to produce contrition in the heart of the sinner.

The minister of God's Word is not taken by surprise when he sees many professing Christ and then defecting. In the stony-ground hearer we have the largest group of professing Christians. Paul prophesied that the last days would be characterized by many "having a form of godliness, but denying the power thereof" (2 Timothy 3:5). They start enthusiastically but they never finish. At first they appear as potential firebrands for God, but like some of those in the church in Sardis they are thought to be spiritually alive, but they are dead (Revelation 3:1). When our Lord had spoken His famous discourse concerning Himself as the living bread who came down from Heaven, "many therefore of His disciples, when they heard this, said, This is an hard saying; who can hear it?... From that time many of His disciples went back, and walked no more with Him" (John 6:60,66).

Our Lord's prophecy in the parable of the stony-ground hearer is being fulfilled before our eyes. Our churches have too many members with stony hearts. They professed joyfully to enter the Christian life, but their interest soon waned. Some of them will put in their appearance at Easter and Christmas, but they have no depth. They are shallow. They are like Gideon's army that numbered 32,000 at first, but then when the going got tough 22,000 quit and returned home. Only 300 stuck it out to the end (Judges 7).

Because the conscience had never been exercised there was no real sense of sin. A religious experience of this nature, touching a sinner merely on the surface of the soul, can result only in apostasy. That crowd who heard Jesus speak this parable had many such professors. Why? Because He led a religious movement that was popular.

The same tragedy is repeating itself today and will continue until Christ returns. Popular religious programs are invading homes throughout America by means of television. They are light, breezy, entertaining, with emotional appeal based on experience. They breed the stony-ground hearer who never experiences genuine Holy Spirit conviction. It is this type of hearer who responds to much of the modern "evangelism" we witness today. Yes, our Lord's prophecy in the parable is being fulfilled.

The Thorny Ground. "And some fell among thorns; and the thorns sprung up, and choked them.... He also that received seed among the thorns is he that heareth the Word; and the care of this world, and the deceitfulness of riches, choke the Word, and he becometh unfruitful" (Matthew 13:7,22). Mark added one thorn, namely, "the lusts of other things" (Mark 4:19). Luke had another addition, namely, the "pleasures of this life" (Luke 8:14).

Here again the seed sown is unproductive. In this third class of hearers the hindrance is not so much the internal condition of the heart as it is external causes. Again our Lord is predicting that the Word preached will not result in a spiritual harvest of souls among all who hear. In the *first* soil, the opposition to the Word was the *devil*; in the *second* the resistance came from the *flesh*; in the *third* the enemy of the Word is the *world*. Here it is that world-system which James called "the enemy of God" (James 4:4).

The thorns in the parable represent the variety of weeds that often choke the good seed, preventing a harvest. Jesus calls them, "the cares of this world." This third hearer is not hardhearted like the first, nor softhearted like the second, but he does have a divided heart. He is trying to do what Jesus said no man can do, namely, "serve God and mammon" (Matthew 6:24). He received the seed but it never bore fruit. He was a spiritual failure. His progress was zero. He is preoccupied with the things of this world. The cares of this world are simply the anxious concerns many professing Christians have for things, some of which may be legitimate in their place, but which dominate one's life so that the Word does not bear fruit.

We see this prophecy of our Lord being fulfilled today. Many professing Christians are preoccupied with home, travel, pleasure, career, making money, striving for success, and a host of other things. They give little or no evidence of having been born again. The heart may be very religious, but it is so engrossed with earthly things that the Word is choked and it produces no fruit. These thorns hinder and harass many of God's dear children. They war against the soul and suppress the Word of God. It is characteristic of our age that many interests in life crowd out the reading and study of the Word of God. Our church rolls carry the names of many persons of this type.

When Jesus visited the home of Mary and Martha, he found in Mary a readiness to sit at His feet and hear His Word. But Martha was cumbered about much service. He rebuked Martha when He said to her, "Thou art careful [anxious] and troubled about *many things*: But *one thing* is needful: and Mary hath chosen that good part, which shall not be taken away from her" (Luke 10:38-42). I have italicized the words *many things* and *one thing*. The Lord Himself was present teaching the Word, sowing His good seed of truth, but the Word was choked in Martha's heart and produced no fruit. Even in the home, a busy housewife, doing a good work, discovers that the thorns have a way of thriving, thereby choking out the Word of God. It is not that any one of us would deliberately deny the Bible or openly reject its message, but we can become so preoccupied with lesser things that we just don't get around to it.

The Good Ground. "But other fell into good ground, and brought forth fruit, some an hundredfold, some sixtyfold, some thirtyfold.... But he that received seed into the good ground is he that heareth the Word, and understandeth it; which also beareth fruit, and bringeth forth, some an hundredfold, some sixty, some thirty" (Matthew 13:8,23).

Any preacher might become discouraged after he sees that seventy-five per cent of the seed sown produced no favorable results. But it is here that we all can take courage and press on, knowing that some of God's Word will fall on good soil and produce a harvest. If the parable is designed to predict the unfavorable response to God's Word during this present dispensation, it is intended also to remind us that there are always those, even though the percentage is not large, who will receive and believe the Word and be saved.

There is plenty of "good ground" in this world. Obviously, there is a lot of evil within man and without, and both sources are militating against the Word of God. However, there is that twenty-five per cent to be reached with the gospel and won to Christ. A harvest of twenty-five per cent is better than no harvest. Everyday we live and move among people presents a golden opportunity to sow the good seed of God's Word. And somewhere along the way there will be those who will "receive it" (Mark 4:20), "keep it" (Luke 8:15), and "understand it" (Matthew 13:23). If we would be fruitful we must be faithful. If we will forget ourselves and our personal interests to serve the Lord, we will reap the harvest. "He that goeth forth and weepeth, bearing precious seed, shall doubtless come again with rejoicing, bringing his sheaves with him" (Psalm 126:6).

Don't allow these first three hearers and their treatment of the truth to defeat you. There will be those who will not receive the message at all, and then there will be those who will receive it superficially. But that is exactly how Jesus said they would respond. We must expect this. "Eyes have they, but they see not; They have ears, but they hear not" (Psalm 135:16-17). The sower is not responsible for the response of the hearer. Nor can the sower make the seed take root and grow. We cannot impart life to spiritually dead people. One can plant and another water, but God only can give the increase (1 Corinthians 3:6).

And let us not be hasty and anxious about quick results. We do not have to see all of the harvest today. One important point in this parable is the proclamation of the truth during this present age. The majority will not receive the Word of God, but a good harvest is certain to follow the sowing of the seed. We must be guided by our Lord's interpretation of this parable, not by a few misguided theologians who hold on to the dream of a world totally converted. The King told us what to expect during His absence. Let us get on with the job, intensify our efforts, and as we sow, make sure that we magnify the Saviour and the Seed, but not the sower. ''And let us not be weary in well doing: for in due season we shall reap, if we faint not'' (Galatians 6:9).

In St. Paul's Cathedral in London there is a stained glass window depicting a man sowing seed. It was presented as a memorial to a man named Samuel A. Burnett. Mr. Burnett devoted his entire lifetime to spreading the Word of God in the wicked East End of London. Beneath the painting there is a plaque which reads, *Dedicated to Samuel A. Burnett, who served in East London for fifty years, and who feared not to sow despite the birds.*

I'll settle for an epitaph like that!

4

THE PARABLE OF THE TARES

Another parable put He forth unto them, saying, The kingdom of heaven is likened unto a man which sowed good seed in his field: But while men slept, his enemy came and sowed tares among the wheat, and went his way. But when the blade was sprung up, and brought forth fruit, then appeared the tares also. So the servants of the householder came and said unto him, Sir, didst not thou sow good seed in thy field? from whence then hath it tares? He said unto them, An enemy hath done this. The servants said unto him, Wilt thou then that we go and gather them up? But he said, Nay; lest while ye gather up the tares, ye root up also the wheat with them.... Then Jesus sent the multitude away, and went into the house: and His disciples came unto Him, saying, Declare unto us the parable of the tares of the field. He answered and said unto them, He that soweth the good seed is the Son of man; The field is the world; the good seed are the children of the kingdom; but the tares are the children of the wicked one; The enemy that sowed them is the devil; the harvest is the end of the world; and the reapers are the angels. As therefore the tares are gathered and burned in the fire; so shall it be in the end of this world. The Son of man shall send forth His angels, and they shall gather out of His kingdom all things that offend, and them which do iniquity; And shall cast them into a furnace of fire: there shall be wailing and gnashing of teeth. Then shall the righteous shine forth as the sun in the kingdom of their Father. Who hath ears to hear, let him hear (Matthew 13:24-29,36-43).

We must keep in mind the fact that there is a con-

sistency in the teaching of our Lord in all seven parables.
The entire chapter in Matthew groups together a series of
parables designed to teach the course and character of this
present age during the King's absence and until He
returns to earth. The King is not now on His earthly
throne, but He is seated at the Father's right hand in
Heaven awaiting the appointed time of His return to earth
to rule.

"The LORD said unto my Lord, Sit thou at My right
hand, until I make Thine enemies Thy footstool" (Psalm
110:1). The parables in Matthew 13 combine to give a
prophetic forecast of conditions on earth during the
present dispensation while the Son is seated at the Father's
right hand.

The first parable teaches clearly that the sowing of the
seed of God's Word will not result in its universal
reception. The majority of those who hear the truth of
God will not receive it to their salvation. The rejection of
God's Word will be greater than its reception. The ex-
travagant expectations of postmillenarians have no basis at
all in the light of our Lord's teaching in this first parable.

The basic character of the present age established in the
first parable is taught clearly in this second parable. In the
parable of the sower it was the condition and character of
the *soils* (human hearts) which hindered the reception of
the good seed of God's Word. In this second parable Jesus
deals with the character of the *seed*. However, this
parable, like the former, refutes conclusively the unscriptural dream that the Church will convert the world.
The earth will be filled with the knowledge of the glory of
the Lord as the waters cover the sea, but not before the

King comes back. As in the first parable, the second tells us why.

Arthur W. Pink, in his treatment of these parables, points out the fact that the number *two* suggests difference and division, being the first number which may be divided. *One* is the number of *unity*. *Two* stands for *division*. In the Biblical account of creation the first statement says, "In the beginning God created the heaven and the earth." Immediately following this we read, "And the earth was [literally, became] without form, and void" (Genesis 1:1-2). The first statement describes the work of God; the second, that of an evil power. And then there follows the fact that "God divided the light from the darkness." The second action, in opposition to the first, brought division. Thus it is in the first two parables in Matthew 13. The first describes the work of Christ; the second the work of Satan.

The parable of the tares is the story of two *seeds*. There is the *good seed* and the *tares* (bad seed) (Matthew 13:24-25). In the first parable, the seed is the Word of God; in the second, the seeds are people. In our Lord's interpretation of the parable He said, "The good seed are the children of the kingdom; but the tares are the children of the wicked one" (13:38). Likewise there are two sowers. "He that sowed the good seed is the Son of man.... The enemy that sowed them [the tares] is the devil" (verses 37,39).

The history of civilization contains the record of the battle of the two seeds. God said to Satan, "And I will put enmity between thee and the woman, and between thy *seed* and her *seed*" (Genesis 3:15). Both *seeds* here refer to people. The serpent's seed does not refer to generations of snakes as yet unhatched. They are men and women, children of the wicked one whose father is the devil. Jesus identified them when He said, "Ye are of your father the devil" (John 8:44). So we have here the posterity or children of Satan on the one hand, and the posterity or children of the woman, on the other. While "the seed of the woman" is principally and primarily Christ (Galatians 3:16), at the same time it must of necessity include all those who are Christ's. The woman, Mary, was the human vessel God used to bring His Son into the world, and now all who have received Him are His spiritual seed. Isaiah prophesied, "When Thou shalt make His soul an offering for sin, He shall see His *seed*, He shall prolong His days, and the pleasure of the LORD shall prosper in His hand" (Isaiah 53:10).

The war between the seeds was predicted by God, and He enunciated the principle that the two seeds are mutually exclusive of, and hostile to, one another. The conflict was occasioned by God Himself for the purpose of maintaining a witness to Himself in a world system dominated by Satan. The issue will finally be settled, not by the subordinates, but between the two principal heads, Christ and Satan. In the meantime the struggle continues, the two seeds being involved, the good seed who are Christ's and the tares who are Satan's.

One important fact must not be overlooked, namely, there is no indication in the Bible that Christ's good seed will ever be anything more than a very small minority. Jesus said to His own, "Fear not, little flock; for it is your Father's good pleasure to give you the kingdom" (Luke

12:32). Notice how Christ calls them His "*little* flock." He tells them not to be anxious about material things, but to seek the kingdom of God. And to those who seek it God will give it to them, and with it He will provide the necessities of life. The fact that we believers are in the minority fits the teaching in the first parable, where only twenty-five per cent of those who heard the Word received and retained it and brought forth fruit.

In the parable of the tares, Satan applies a different method in his opposition to the King and His kingdom. Here he turns farmer to play the role of an imitator. The Lord Jesus sows seed, so now he too will sow seed. Remember, Satan is never an innovator but always an imitator. His counterfeits are people, his own attempted reproduction of the people of God. While the Lord is sowing the good seed who are His children, Satan is sowing tares who are his children. The counterfeit is in appearance so much like the genuine the two are not distinguishable.

Now exactly who are the tares? They are not only the drug addicts, alcoholics, prostitutes, thieves, and murderers. These are all the children of the devil and are known as such, but they are not imitating the children of God's kingdom. Were they the tares in Christ's parable, the servants of the householder could uproot them and not root up some wheat with them. Obviously, there is a distinction between immoral, indecent people and the people of God.

When Satan sows his seed he imitates the good seed. It was to the religious intelligensia, the scribes and Pharisees, that Jesus spoke when He said, "Ye are of your father the devil" (John 8:44). They were the ones upon whom Christ pronounced severe judgment, calling them "hypocrites" and "blind" (Matthew 23:13-33). Fifteen times in Matthew's Gospel Jesus used the word "hypocrite," which means a play actor or stage actor, the person whose dress, make-up, and voice are not those of the real person himself. Actually, he is playing the part of another. Such are the tares in the parable. They are Satan's children presenting themselves as the children of God. And why are they doing this? Jesus said they are "blind." Their minds are blinded by Satan (Romans 11:25; 2 Corinthians 3:14; 4:4).

This is the mystery of the kingdom. Satan's biggest operation is in religion. He infiltrates with his children, who pose as Christians, but who are spurious, false, counterfeit. Outwardly and superficially they appear as Christians, but they are fraudulent. Yes, Satan is in the business of religion and he has his imitation church. His children preach "another Jesus" and "another gospel" (2 Corinthians 11:4), a gospel of another kind, different from the gospel of Jesus Christ (Galatians 1:6-7). Satan *fashions* his ministers, that is, he trains them to act and speak like the ministers of Jesus Christ (2 Corinthians 11:13-15). They assume all of the characteristics of Christ's ministers of righteousness, when in reality they are ministers of Satan.

Paul encountered just such a person in Elymas (Acts 13:10). The parable does not tell us that the enemy sowed briars or thorns or thistles. All such would be easily identified. What he did sow was a degenerate wheat not perceptible to the most skilled farmer. Our Lord told how the last days would be marked by growing satanic deception (Matthew 24:4-5,11,24). "We are not ignorant of his devices" (2 Corinthians 2:11).

Our Lord has warned His disciples to "beware of false prophets, which come to you in sheep's clothing, but inwardly they are ravening wolves" (Matthew 7:15). Judas was a tare among the wheat, a child of the devil mingling with the children of Christ's kingdom. For nearly three years he passed himself off as a true son of God and could not be distinguished by Christ's disciples (John 13:18-30). Some of those wolves in sheep's clothing had gotten into the assembly in Ephesus (Acts 20:28-31). They did not come howling like a wolf tracking down its prey; they came in sheep's clothing. Both Peter (2 Peter 2:1) and Jude (verses 3-4) warned of the coming of Satan's children. Yes, even in the early Church a few tares did creep in.

But where must we expect to find this mixture of believers and unbelievers, saved and unsaved, "children of the kingdom" and "children of the wicked one"? When our Lord interpreted the parable He said, "The field is the world" (Matthew 13:38). The field is not the Church. Matthew 13 is not dealing specifically with the Church nor the church age between Pentecost and the Rapture. The period in this passage is bounded at each end by the first and second advents of Christ to the earth. Now the church age is included in that period, but the Church particularly and precisely is not in view at all.

Those who hold to the erroneous view that the kingdom is the Church want us to believe that the Church should tolerate false doctrine and other forms of impurity until

Christ returns. We can only reply with our Lord's words, "The field is the world," not the Church. All impurities, whether in doctrine or deportment, must be disciplined in the Church. Discipline in the churches is taught in the New Testament (1 Corinthians 5:4-10; 2 Corinthians 2:6-7). The harvest time for the world, when believers will be separated from unbelievers, is "the end of the age" (Matthew 13:39). In the meantime, the children of the kingdom must continue to sow the seed of God's Word and live separated lives (Psalm 122; Romans 12:2; 1 Corinthians 5:11; 2 Corinthians 6:14-18). We should not be perplexed when we view increased satanic activity in the world because we know the *time* of the harvest will come at the "consummation of the age" (Matthew 13:39 RV margin).

At times it becomes a bit disturbing to see and hear appeals to join with this group or that and help "change the world" for Christ. In the first place, the Church is never told to change the world. The Church's business is to go into all the world and make known the gospel of Christ, leading people to know and receive the Lord Jesus as their Saviour. God is not now changing the world; He is *calling* out from the world "a people for His name" (Acts 15:14). Furthermore, Christ will not need any assistance when He is ready to change the world. After His rejection He said, "My kingdom is not of this world" (John 18:36). When He comes to earth again, then will come to pass the prophecy, "The kingdoms of this world are become the kingdoms of our Lord, and of His Christ; and He shall reign for ever and ever" (Revelation 11:15). When the meaning of these parables is understood, we will have our priorities straight.

Recently a Christian leader of national reputation promoted the idea that if we could get Christians elected to political positions our national problems could be solved. Even if the president of the United States, every congressman, every senator, every governor, and every mayor in America were Christians, our problems could not be solved. We are still in the world where Satan has his tares. The whole idea of changing the world for Christ is the creation of man's imagination, a fantasy without any Biblical basis.

The first Sower in this parable is Christ Himself. He is that "man which sowed good seed in *His* field" (Matthew 13:24). It is *His*. The whole of the ordered universe, including the earth and its inhabitants, is His creation. He claims ownership of all. "The earth is the Lord's, and the fullness thereof; the world, and they that dwell therein" (Psalm 24:1). The devil is a squatter, sitting on land that is not his. He is here now scattering his tares among the wheat, mingling his counterfeits with the genuine. He will continue to imitate until "the end of the age." The children of the King are exhorted to "put on the whole armour of God, that ye may be able to stand against the wiles of the devil" (Ephesians 6:11). As we wear our armor, no harm can come to us even though we are surrounded on every side by the enemy's tares.

Before concluding the study on the parable of the tares, I would have you share with me a thought or two as to the time the enemy sowed tares. Jesus said, "While men slept, His enemy came and sowed tares among the wheat" (Matthew 13:25). It is a night scene, suggesting that Satan's activities are not performed in the open. He works best under cover of darkness. What a challenge to us Christians that we do not lapse into a state of spiritual sleep or lethargy! Jesus said, "Ye are the light of the world.... Let your light so shine before men, that they may see your good works, and glorify your Father which is in heaven" (Matthew 5:14,16). "Ye are all the children of light, and the children of the day: we are not of the night, nor of darkness. Therefore let us not sleep, as do others; but let us watch and be sober" (1 Thessalonians 5:5-6).

5

THE PARABLE OF THE MUSTARD SEED

Another parable put He forth unto them, saying, The kingdom of heaven is like a grain of mustard seed, which a man took, and sowed in his field: Which, indeed, is the least of all seeds; but when it is grown, it is the greatest among herbs, and becometh a tree, so that the birds of the air come and lodge in the branches of it (Matthew 13:31-32).

The student of these parables is confronted with a very real problem at this point. The first two parables, the sower and the tares, were explained by our Lord. His explanation was clear enough so that the meaning He attached to them could not be mistaken or misunderstood. But here in the parable of the mustard seed, Jesus says nothing about its meaning, the student being on his own in search of it. And yet, in the strictest sense, we are not left to our own reasoning and interpretation.

Dr. G. Campbell Morgan began his exposition of this parable by reminding his readers of a peril to be avoided in its interpretation. He cautioned against "the peril of popularity," that is, being influenced by the general consensus of expository opinion. Popular interpretation is not necessarily the correct one, nor is it a guarantee of accuracy. For example, almost one hundred years ago, in 1882 to be exact, the popular and respected theologian Alexander Balmain Bruce published his 500-page book entitled, *The Parabolic Teaching of Christ*. Dr. Bruce saw in the parable of the mustard seed "a good omen of the future, in which Jesus foreshadowed the growth of His kingdom from its small beginnings to a great magnitude.... It will one day be an institution which the world can no longer treat with disdain ... it is intended in the parable to represent the spread of Christianity as of a miraculous character."

Dr. Bruce's interpretation has become the popular one. The majority of expositors follow him in the belief that, even though the first two parables show the truth of God rejected, and Satan infiltrating the world with his children, "by the parable of the mustard seed, Jesus is teaching that all is not lost. His kingdom will spread and flourish and ultimately triumph." How good and gifted teachers of God's Word can turn this parable completely upside down is a sad wonder! I cannot accept this interpretation. I will try to tell you why.

First of all, it must be borne in mind that there is harmony in the teaching in these parables. Whatever difference there might be in the figures of speech our Lord used, there is consistency in the interpretation. The seven parables form a connected and completed whole. In my judgment, this is a basic principle of interpretation in studying these parables. Any interpretation of one of them which contradicts that of any other cannot be the correct interpretation. Therefore, I must proceed to interpret this third parable on the same basis established by our Lord in His explanation of the first two. This leads me to the conclusion that the popular interpretation which makes the parable of the mustard seed to teach the success of

Christ's kingdom in all the world during His absence is an incorrect one.

We have in this parable an unnatural, and therefore an unhealthy development. A mustard seed does not normally grow into a healthy tree producing its fruit for the benefit of mankind. The mustard is an herb, not a tree. An herb developing into a tree is something unknown in the natural world. The herb and the tree are two different species, and there is never any crossing over between the two. The Biblical account of creation states this in unmistakably clear language, for we read, "And the earth brought forth grass, and *herb* yielding seed *after his kind*, and the *tree* yielding fruit, whose seed was in itself, *after his kind*: and God saw that it was good" (Genesis 1:12). The italics are mine for the purpose of drawing attention to the fact that each, the herb and the tree, can reproduce only *after his kind*. What we have in this parable is a perverted growth, and it is not good.

We have then here another movement comparable to that in the preceding parables. In the first parable the greater growth is among those who reject the truth rather than among those who receive it. In the second parable Satan's seed, those who rejected the Word of God imitate in *appearance* those who received the truth and were thereby born again into the kingdom of God. It follows that the imitation is of a religious nature. Here in the third parable, the mustard seed, we are given to see the two, believers and counterfeit believers, in one big monstrosity. I can think of no better descriptive term for this religious abnormality than *Christendom*. It is not *Christianity*; it is an imitation of Christianity, but it is religious.

The greatness that developed in the mustard seed becoming a tree is a false greatness. It is characterized by ecumenicity, numbers, influence, and wealth. We see a type of that large spreading tree in Daniel 4. Nebuchadnezzar had received from God the local earthly kingdom of Babylon, but in the hands of the godless king it was corrupted! One night Nebuchadnezzar dreamed a dream. He said:

> Thus were the visions of mine head in my bed; I saw, and behold a tree in the midst of the earth, and the height thereof was great. The tree grew, and was strong, and the height thereof reached unto heaven, and the sight thereof *to the end of all the earth*: The leaves thereof were fair, and the fruit thereof much, and in it was meat for all: the beasts of the field had shadow under it, and the fowls of the heaven dwelt in the boughs thereof, and all flesh was fed of it. I saw in the visions of my head upon my bed, and, behold, a watcher and an holy one came down from heaven; He cried aloud, and said thus, Hew down the tree, and cut off its branches; shake off its leaves, and scatter its fruit; let the beasts get away from under it, and the fowls from its branches. Nevertheless, leave the stump of its roots in the earth, even with a band of iron and bronze, in the tender grass of the field; and let him be wet with the dew of heaven, and let his portion be with the beasts in the grass of the earth. Let his heart be changed from man's, and let a beast's heart be given unto him; and let seven times pass over him. This matter is by the decree of the watchers, and the demand by the word of the holy ones, to the intent that the living may know that the Most High ruleth in the kingdom of men, and giveth it to whomsoever He will, and setteh up over it the basest of men (Daniel 4:10-17).

After the Egyptian magicians, astrologers, and soothsayers had failed in their efforts to interpret the dream, Daniel appeared. He said to the Babylonian monarch:

The tree that thou sawest, which grew, and was strong, whose height reached unto the heaven, and the sight of it *to all the earth*, Whose leaves were fair, and its fruit much, and in it was meat for all; under which the beasts of the field dwelt, and upon whose branches the fowls of the heavens had their habitation: It is thou, O king, that art grown and become strong; for thy greatness is grown, and reacheth unto heaven, and thy dominion *to the end of the earth* (Daniel 4:20-22).

Both in the dream and in its interpretation one sees the ecumenical significance of the tree, "to the end of all the earth" (4:11,22).

There is a close parallel here to Christ's parable. The tree was a figure of a kingdom giving shelter to the birds. In the parable of the sower the birds represent Satan and his agents (Matthew 13:19; Mark 4:15; Luke 8:12). The word "fowls" is not always used in a bad sense. In several passages the "dove" represents that which is good. But there can be no mistaking their meaning in these parables. The action of the fowls illustrates the work of Satan. There is a picture in the Bible of the collapse of ecclesiastical Babylon when Christ returns to establish His kingdom. The Apostle John wrote, "And after these things I saw another angel come down from heaven, having great power; and the earth was lighted with his glory. And he cried mightily with a strong voice, saying, Babylon the great is fallen, is fallen, and is become the habitation of devils [i.e., demons], and the hold of every foul spirit, and a cage of every unclean and hateful bird" (Revelation 18:1-2). By no stretch of the imagination can the tree in the parable of the mustard seed represent that which is good.

Today it is the "in thing" to say you are *born again*. Many people are being born again, and this is cause for rejoicing. But then a person's merely saying he is born again does not make it so. Paul warned Timothy, "Now the Spirit speaketh expressly, that in the latter times some shall depart from the faith, giving heed to seducing spirits, and doctrines of devils [demons]" (1 Timothy 4:1). When Satan learned that he could not prevent God's Word from saving some, he began to imitate the children of God. His imitation has been so close and clever that many are jumping on his religious bandwagon. And it is ever growing in size. Numbers are equated with rightness. Bigness is equated with blessing.

Today we are witnessing renewed efforts to establish the glory of the tree through the ecumenical church. The coming world church continues to grow, spreading its branches and inviting all who will to unite with it. This parable teaches us that as the age draws to a close many will be drawn to the great tree. This corrupt religious system affords a shelter for the devil and his children. Organized religion offers a shelter for men and women who do not believe the basic doctrines of historic Christianity as they are declared in the Bible.

When a new approach loses its appeal, Satan comes forward with a different one. This is quite noticeable in the religious world. Just a few years ago we awakened one morning to an alarming bit of theological mumbo jumbo under the caption, "God is dead." Fortunately, it didn't last long enough for publishing houses to print and peddle their wares and reap a money harvest. They never got to the bank on that one. It is interesting to me that the morticians who were loudest in honking their latest corpse are strangely silent. Now that the world knows that God is very much alive and well, Satan has gone to the other extreme. God is supposed to be the driving force behind the action and activities in all the latest religious movements.

The latest religious movement with a strong ecumenical appeal is the modern charismatic cult. It has drawn into its tree birds of every religious description. Since 1950 the charismatic ecumenical tree, with its wide-spreading branches, has attracted Roman Catholics, Mormons, Seventh Day Adventists, Jehovah's Witnesses, and protestants from every denomination, and I am sure that among them will be found a few of the Lord's "little flock." But many of them have not the slightest idea of what it means to be born again.

In the parable of the mustard seed, the tree symbolizes growth, greatness, and prominence. Judged by the world's standards, its size and influence make it important so that now it is popular to find shelter in this religious monstrosity. Even the worldly and the wealthy are being drawn to it. We can see here a kingdom spreading and flourishing, but it is not the kingdom of God.

The "little flock" does not dominate in its natural setting. The secret of the power of Christ's true Church is faith in her Head. He said, "I will build My church; and the gates of hell shall not prevail against it" (Matthew 16:18). The inner characteristic of its members is humility. The true children of His kingdom must be able to say and demonstrate as did John, "He must increase, but I must decrease" (John 3:30). It was this spirit of self-renunciation in John which led Jesus to say of him, "For I say unto you, Among those that are born of women there is not a greater prophet than John the Baptist: but he that is least in the kingdom of God is greater than he" (Luke 7:28).

One of the basic lessons taught in this parable is the faith principle. Jesus said, "If ye have faith as a grain of mustard seed, ye shall say unto this mountain, Remove hence to yonder place; and it shall remove; and nothing shall be impossible unto you" (Matthew 17:20). The faith principle is basic to a man's relation to God, and it is also the principle by which the children of God live from day to day. "The just shall live by faith" (Romans 1:17; Galatians 3:11; Hebrews 10:38). "For we walk by faith, not by sight" (2 Corinthians 5:7). It is at this point that God's true Church and Satan's ecumenical church part. This little mustard seed illustrates the principle of living by faith.

6

THE PARABLE OF THE LEAVEN

Another parable spoke He unto them; The kingdom of heaven is like unto leaven, which a woman took, and hid in three measures of meal, till the whole was leavened (Matthew 13:33).

Diametrically opposed to one another are two accepted interpretations of the parable of the leaven. It is possible that more controversy has revolved around the explanation of this verse than around any other single verse in the Bible. One interpretation is that the leaven in the parable is a symbol of good, teaching that the gospel will permeate and pervade the entire human race until all mankind is converted to Jesus Christ. The other interpretation is the direct opposite and teaches that leaven in this verse, as everywhere else in Scripture, is a recognized principle of evil. Obviously, both interpretations cannot be correct.

More than one hundred years ago the late Dean Henry Alford adopted the theory that the leaven in Christ's parable was the gospel, penetrating the whole mass of humanity by degrees, by the power of the Holy Spirit. He saw in this parable a prophetic view of a converted world, brought to pass by the gospel advancing secretly and gradually into the whole of the race of mankind. The venerable dean saw Christ's kingdom advancing to worldwide dimensions effecting a total social transformation. It sounded good, and so, many of his students believed it and continued to propagate it. However, two world wars, plus more than a dozen major conflicts in Asia and the Middle East, plus continual upheavals in Africa have reduced considerably the ranks of those who fail to see in the parable of the leaven that which our Lord intended to teach, namely, the progress of deterioration and corruption. History disproves the leaven to be an influence for good, purifying the whole.

Inasmuch as all seven parables are designed to set forth the trend of the age during our Lord's absence from the earth, and leading up to His return, the teaching throughout must be consistent. If the leaven is the gospel healing the whole of society, then the parable of the leaven is out of harmony with the teaching in those parables which preceded it. How can the whole be leavened for good if only twenty-five per cent of those who hear the Word of God receive it and produce fruit? How can the whole be leavened for good when the tares (the devil's children) remain to the end of the age? How can the whole be leavened for good as long as the fowls (the emissaries of Satan) find lodging in the tree of Christendom? As long as there are buzzards in the branches of the organized church, there will be opposition to the Word of God.

Leaven corrupts the pure gospel of the grace of God. As the parable of the mustard seed shows the outward, visible growth of organized religion, so the parable of the leaven reveals the internal "hidden" corruption of that religious monstrosity. It was not the intention of our Lord in these parables to teach the triumph of the gospel in this age, but rather the workings of Satan in his opposition to the gospel.

I reject totally the once popular view that the leaven represents the gospel and its power. I reject it because it cannot be substantiated by the Word of God. If the promoters of this incorrect interpretation cannot see its fallacy by the historical evidence of a deteriorating society, they should be able to see it in the Bible. But they are victims of their own wishful thinking. To them it is unthinkable that there might be corruption in a society where Jesus Christ has planted His Church. But our Lord Himself said that, as the age runs it course and His coming again draws near, corruption of all sorts would prevail. The leaven of corruption will appear in growing deception, wars, murders, hate, betrayal, iniquity, and much more (Matthew 24). What was at one time the most popular interpretation of this parable is incorrect. You may rest assured that the standards and principles of Christianity will never be universally accepted before the return of Jesus Christ to the earth.

If leaven is the gospel permeating and pervading the whole world and Christianizing all of society, then it has not succeeded. It is now almost two thousand years since our Lord spoke this parable. If leaven is the gospel transforming the world from evil to good, then we should expect to see the world just about converted to Jesus Christ. If this is what our Lord meant, then He was mistaken, and every true minister and missionary of the gospel has been misled. I have given almost fifty years of my life in preparation for the ministry and the preaching of God's Word. If leaven is the gospel bringing in the golden age, I have wasted my life and I would be the most discouraged and disappointed man alive today. But I am not discouraged, and the gospel has not failed. Jesus never taught at any time that the preaching of the gospel would result in the conversion of the whole world.

This incorrect interpretation of the parable of the leaven is in reality the doctrine of universalism, which means that all will eventually be saved. The prevailing mind of universalism is currently sweeping a large religious segment of Africa. And yet the United Presbyterians announced a cut of over a million dollars in their missionary budget and the enforced withdrawal of two hundred twenty missionaries, all in one year (1972), due to a sharp drop in denominational income. Universalism is an excellent tool for uniting people of different religions, but such a union is producing the mustard tree with every foul bird in its branches. The number of people yet to be won to Christ in Africa has more than doubled since 1900, and will be more than tripled by the year 2000. If leaven is the gospel to save *the whole* world, when will "the whole" be leavened? The whole idea seems absurd, at least to this writer.

Please believe me when I tell you I have no cause to champion except that of the truth of the Scriptures, the Word of God. It is to that Word I invite your prayerful attention.

Leaven in the Old Testament

The first reference to leaven in the Old Testament is in Genesis 19. When God's messenger visited Lot in Sodom, we are told that "he made them a feast, and did bake unleavened bread, and they did eat" (verse 3). Note the specific mention that leaven was omitted from the bread. No doubt leaven was commonly used in that wicked city. We are not told why Lot did not bake the bread with leaven, but it is obvious that he knew he shouldn't.

The next reference to leaven is in connection with Israel's redemption from Egypt. The Passover lamb was to be slain and its blood applied to the two sideposts and the upper doorpost of the houses. Then on the night before their departure from the land of bondage (Egypt), the Israelites were to "eat the flesh ... roast with fire and *unleavened* bread" (Exodus 12:8). In years to come Israel was to celebrate their deliverance with an annual memorial feast, a celebration which was to last seven days. During that entire week leaven was to be removed from every Jewish house. The people were instructed to eat only unleavened bread (Exodus 12:15,17-20).

It is significant that the first mention of leaven, a symbol of corruption, is traced to Sodom and Egypt, two locations whose inhabitants were known for evil and their opposition to Jehovah and His people. And it is no mere accident that both Sodom and Egypt are associated with the evil of Satan and his man of sin when they murder God's two witnesses during the tribulation (Revelation 11:8). If leaven is a type of that which is good, why would God command His people to remove it entirely from their houses during the Passover season?

Leaven was excluded from all blood offerings and sacrificial offerings made by fire. God said, "Thou shalt not offer the blood of My sacrifice with *leaven*" (Exodus

34:25). Explicit instructions were given concerning the meal offering that it should not be baked with leaven nor eaten with leaven (Leviticus 2:11; 6:14-17). The reason for this prohibition is obvious. These offerings were a type of the perfect sacrifice of the sinless Son of God, our Lord Jesus Christ. ''For even Christ our passover is sacrificed for us'' (1 Corinthians 5:7). The presence of the leaven (or yeast) started a process of fermentation resulting in corruption, therefore it was forbidden of all offerings in which Christ was prefigured. Only unleavened cakes were permitted on the altar of Jehovah (Leviticus 10:12). All types of Christ must be pure, for ''in Him is no sin'' (1 John 3:5). *Leaven* is a figure of corruption.

Our study of Old Testament passages dealing with leaven would be incomplete if we overlooked the meal offering in which leaven was permitted. God gave to Moses the following order:

> And ye shall count unto you from the next day after the sabbath, from the day that ye brought the sheaf of the wave offering; seven sabbaths shall be complete: Even unto the next day after the seventh sabbath shall ye number fifty days; and ye shall offer a new meal offering unto the LORD. Ye shall bring out of your habitations two wave loaves of two tenth parts; they shall be of fine flour; they shall be baked with leaven; they are the first fruits unto the LORD (Leviticus 23:15-17).

Why were the two wave loaves of the Pentecostal offering baked with leaven? Some folks would have us believe that here leaven is symbolic of something good. But again they are mistaken. We know that Passover was fulfilled at Calvary in the death of Christ (1 Corinthians 5:7). The next feast, The Feast of Weeks, held fifty days later, foreshadowed Pentecost. On the Day of Pentecost the Church was formed (Acts 2), believing Jew and believing Gentile being baptized into the Body of Christ (1 Corinthians 12:13). Those born-again ones were the "first fruits" of the new dispensation. The two loaves prefigured the two classes, Jew and Gentile, now made one in Christ (Ephesians 2:14-16).

But even though the Christian is born of the Holy Spirit and indwelt by the Spirit, the sin principle is still in him. The Adamic nature is never totally eradicated in this life. The leaven of the flesh is present in each believer. Paul recognized the presence of leaven in himself when he testified, "For I know that in me (that is, in my flesh,) dwelleth no good thing" (Romans 7:18). The Church in her present state on earth, awaiting her Lord's appearing, is not perfect. So often the members allow the flesh to dominate, and division and strife result. As we examine leaven in the New Testament we will see how it crept into the early Church in its various forms of worldliness, formalism, hypocrisy, materialism, immorality, and legalism. When bread typifies Christ it is *unleavened*, free from all taint of putrefaction and corruption, for He is the Living Bread which came down from Heaven (John 6:48-51). When bread typifies man, even at his best, it is always *leavened*.

Leaven in the New Testament

In the New Testament the words *leaven* and *unleavened* appear not less than seventeen times. In every instance except one it denotes that which is evil. The one exception where it is not designated good or bad is in this parable.

However, I know of no principle of Biblical interpretation, exegetical or contextual, that will permit a change of meaning in the symbolism in Matthew 13:33. Ancient Jews used the word *leaven* to indicate "evil affections and naughtiness of the heart." Greek historians said, "Leaven is both itself generated by corruption, and also corrupts the mass with which it is mingled." These views are consistent with both the Old and New Testament.

The Leaven of the Pharisees

After our Lord gave the parable of the leaven He followed it up with a warning to His disciples, "Take heed and beware of the leaven of the Pharisees and of the Sadducees" (Matthew 16:6). What did He mean by the leaven of the Pharisees? Luke wrote, "He began to say unto His disciples first of all, Beware ye of the leaven of the Pharisees, which is hypocrisy" (Luke 12:1). The Pharisees believed a man was very religious and thereby pleased God if he maintained a right appearance outwardly before the eyes of his fellowmen. The heart might be filled with jealousy, envy, covetousness, lust, bitterness, and hatred, but as long as he maintained a correct appearance externally he was a good man.

The hypocrite is an actor, a pretender. He looks and plays the part of another. On the surface he impresses others with his goodness, but in his heart there is that degrading and deadly bit of leaven working secretly and insidiously. The hypocrite enjoys the praises and plaudits of men who consider him to be pious and spiritual, but his outward actions are merely a mask, a false guise (Matthew

6:1-6,16-18). That is the leaven of hypocrisy.

The hypocrite is quick to detect the slightest defect in others while he is blind to his own weaknesses and faults. He will notice at great distance a splinter (mote) in his brother's eye, but be totally oblivious to the telephone pole (beam) protruding from his own eye (Matthew 7:5; Luke 6:42). That is the leaven of hypocrisy.

The hypocrite is not an atheist, nor irreligious. To the contrary, he is most punctilious in matters pertaining to religion. But his religion is nothing more than an outward show controlled by the traditions of men. His worship is based on form and ceremonies but his heart is far from God (Matthew 15:1-20). That is the leaven of hypocrisy.

The longest and most detailed picture of the leaven of the Pharisees was presented by our Lord in Matthew 23. It is well to read that chapter aloud from time to time. I read it frequently. It contains the most vivid expose of the leaven of the Pharisees and the most scathing denunciation to come from the lips of our Lord. After reading that chapter one must conclude that if Christ's parable of the leaven is a type of that which is good, then He deliberately confused His disciples.

The Leaven of the Sadducees

Our Lord said to His disciples, "Take heed and beware of the leaven of the Pharisees and of the Sadducees" (Matthew 16:6). Observing that the disciples did not understand His statement, He followed through with these words, "How is it that ye do not understand that I spoke not to you concerning bread, but that ye should

beware of the leaven of the Pharisees and of the Sadducees? Then understood they that He made them not to
beware of the leaven of bread, but of the doctrine of the
Pharisees and of the Sadducees'' (Matthew 16:11-12).

What did Jesus mean by ''the doctrine of the Sadducees''? Matthew says, ''The same day came to Him the
Sadducees, which say that there is no resurrection''
(Matthew 22:23). Even after Pentecost the Sadducees were
disturbed when Peter and John ''preached through Jesus
the resurrection from the dead'' (Acts 4:1-2). These same
Sadducees had the apostles imprisoned, showing the
extent of their hatred for the Christian teaching on the
resurrection and life after death. The doctrine of the
Sadducees is further clarified by Luke when he wrote, ''For
the Sadducees say that there is no resurrection, neither
angel, nor spirit'' (Acts 23:8).

The leaven of the Sadducees was the doctrine of
humanistic materialism, that life consists only of those
things one can see and touch and taste and smell and hear.
They were the existentialists of their time. They
rationalized that a man must live for the present, that
there is nothing beyond this life. Actually, they denied
the supernatural. In their denial of spirit beings they were
atheistic, since God is spirit (John 4:24). This second most
powerful party in Jewry were the Jewish materialists of
their day.

We can see the leaven of the Sadducees in the Church
today. These materialists have their posterity. Some of
them wear the cloth of the clergy but deny the supernatural, or they attempt to explain away the miracles
recorded in the Word of God. This is the leaven of

humanism with its social gospel. They have been admitted as members into many of the churches and have been appointed as elders, deacons, trustees, and Sunday school teachers. And now we are seeing the fruit of that leaven in the apostasy within the churches. There are active church members who have never been saved, men and women who have not been born again.

Jesus said that the leaven of the Sadducees was a corrupt and corrupting doctrine. It is noticed, not in what they say, but more often in what they do not say. They will not affirm their faith in the fundamental doctrines of true historic Christianity as recorded in the Word of God. Dr. J. J. Van Gorder told about a sign over a woodworker's shop which read, ''All kinds of twisting and turning done here.'' That would be a fitting sign to hang from some pulpits. With tongue in cheek these double-talk artists aim at nothing and hit it every time. The leaven in the meal introduces a principle of deterioration and disintegration. The history of nineteen centuries proves this to be so.

The Leaven of Herod

Jesus charged His disciples, ''Take heed, beware of the leaven of ... Herod'' (Mark 8:15). From other Scriptures we know that the Herodians were in league with the Pharisees (Matthew 22:16; Mark 3:6; 12:13). This tells us they opposed Christ and His message. Those followers of Herod were clever politicians ever trying to win the favor of their king and leader. They were a worldly lot.

Can there be any doubt in our minds that leaven is a

corrupting influence in the Church? Are we blind to the fact that there is a psuedo-Christianity, "having a form of godliness, but denying the power thereof?" (2 Timothy 3:5) If those venerable saints of past centuries, who believed that leaven is the pure gospel converting all of mankind, were alive today they would not believe and teach their erroneous doctrine.

Herod Antipas was a licentious man who induced the wife of his own brother to live with him in adultery. He was a wicked and revengeful man who had John the Baptist imprisoned and later murdered because he reproved the king for his immorality. So cunning and deceitful was Herod that our Lord called him a fox (Luke 13:31-33).

The leaven of Herod has never been eradicated. It is with us today. Worldliness in its various forms has crept into the Church. Paul faced it in the church at Corinth. He cites the case of a young man who was actually living in incest with his stepmother. The apostle wrote, "Your glorying is not good. Know ye not that a little leaven leaveneth the whole lump? Purge out, therefore, the old leaven, that ye may be a new lump, as ye are unleavened. For even Christ, our passover, is sacrificed for us. Therefore, let us keep the feast, not with old leaven, neither with the leaven of malice and wickedness, but with the unleavened bread of sincerity and truth" (1 Corinthians 5:6-8). If our Lord ever intended leaven to be a type of good, Paul had no knowledge of it. The church in Corinth had within its membership those carnal professing Christians whose lives were influenced by the leaven of Herod.

Paul admonished the Church to *purge out the leaven*. He is telling the Church to dismiss the incestuous man before his wicked way of life should lead others to follow him. Paul's statement that believers are unleavened should settle the matter once and for all time as to the typical significance of leaven. According to Paul, leaven was a symbol of evil that had worked itself inside the Church. It is the leaven of worldliness and carnality in the Church which is robbing her of spiritual power. Some churches do nothing to discourage divorce and remarriage, illegitimacy, abortion, homosexuality, drinking of alcoholic beverages, and the like. We had better heed the warning of Jesus when He said, "Beware of the leaven of Herod."

The last passage in which leaven is mentioned in the New Testament is Galatians 5:7-9. Paul wrote, "Ye did run well; who did hinder you that ye should not obey the truth? This persuasion cometh not of him that calleth you. A little leaven leaventh the whole lump." Leaven here represents a form of doctrinal error, an attempt to mix law and grace. This is the leaven of legalism. There were false teachers who entered in among the Christians in the churches in the province of Galatia. Those legalizers taught that it was necessary to keep the Mosaic Law, circumcision in particular, as an essential ingredient for salvation. Paul called it a "persuasion," that which could exert a strong influence to "hinder" (meaning, to drive back). And then he added, "It cometh not of Him that calleth you" (verses 7-8).

These first four parables in Matthew 13 contain proof that no millennium of blessedness can appear on the earth between the first and second advents of Christ. And if someone objects that Jesus would not liken the kingdom of Heaven to that which is evil, it is sufficient to reply that He did liken that aspect of the kingdom of Heaven in Matthew 13 to include both wheat and tares, good and bad fish. I merely remind the objectors that they have failed to see that the kingdom in these parables does not mean Heaven nor the Church. Then too, it should be noted that when Christ returns to earth and sets up His literal kingdom, evil will not be absent totally. At the beginning of the millennium all who enter will have been saved. However, during those thousand years, millions will be born, many of whom will not accept the Lord Jesus Christ in their hearts. True, they will be subject to Him, but only because He shall rule them with a rod of iron (Revelation 19:15). True, every knee shall bow and every tongue shall confess that Jesus Christ is Lord (Philippians 2:10-11), but many of them will do so only because they have no choice. After the millennium, when Satan is loosed from his incarceration he will go out and deceive the nation (Revelation 20:7-8). Those whom Satan deceives will not be truly born again, the many who were born during the millennium and who did not receive Christ in their hearts. During the literal kingdom of Christ on earth the leaven will be present in the hearts of some.

The Meaning of the Meal

Again we must look in Scripture for the meaning of *"three measures of meal."* I have not found this expression anywhere else in the New Testament. We must turn to the Old Testament to learn its meaning. Keep in mind the fact that when Jesus employed the term, *three measures of meal*, He used a Bible term.

Those commentators who interpret the leaven to be the gospel, make the meal to mean humanity. Therefore, hiding the leaven of the gospel in the meal of humanity, the result will be the conversion of all humanity to Jesus Christ. We have sought to show earlier in this chapter that such an interpretation is not the correct one. Meal in Scripture represents that which is good, but the Scripture nowhere teaches that humanity is good. On the contrary, God's Word says, "There is none that doeth good, no, not one" (Romans 3:12). The meal does not symbolize the human race.

It is often helpful to the student of the Bible to locate where in Scripture a word or phrase appears the first time. This has been called "the law of first mention." The first time the phrase "three measures of meal" appears in the Scriptures is in Genesis 18. Abraham was in his home with his wife Sarah. They had erected their tent in an oak grove at Mamre. One day three visitors approached the tent. Abraham greeted them and recognized One of them to be more than human. That day God Himself had visited Abraham. It was one of several preincarnate appearances of our Lord recorded in the Old Testament. Such an appearance is called a theophany. Before ever the Bible was written, God would appear to man to bring to him some special revelation. This was one of those rare visits. Abraham and Sarah, then past that time of life to bear children of their own, were to become parents of a son (Genesis 18:9-15). God had visited this aged couple to convey to them the good news.

While Abraham talked with the visitors, Sarah prepared "three measures of fine meal" and baked cakes. So the phrase was first used in connection with preparing a meal. Abraham and Sarah were sharing what they had. It was a way of communicating, or fellowshiping with their guests. In that instance they were fellowshiping with God. Meal, then, is a picture of believers having fellowship with God and with each other. This oneness with God is a very precious fellowship. In the ritual of the Hebrew people the meal offering symbolized their dedication to Jehovah and to serving Him.

And this is what Christianity is all about. When a believing sinner is born again it is like being initiated into a new fellowship. "God is faithful, by whom ye were called unto the *fellowship* of His Son, Jesus Christ our Lord" (1 Corinthians 1:9). Those Christians at Corinth needed to learn the great lesson that they were called by God to share together the life of Jesus Christ. The Apostle John wrote, "That which we have seen and hear declare we unto you, that ye also may have fellowship with us: and truly our fellowship is with the Father, and with His Son Jesus Christ" (1 John 1:3). There is a unique commonness of life that is shared by the people of God. It commences with one being rightly related to God and it continues among Christians being rightly related to each other.

In our Lord's parable the woman acts deceitfully by secretly introducing the corrupting influence of leaven into the meal. From the earliest days of the Christian Church the fellowship of believers has been fractured by action both from within and without. In Corinth the leaven of carnality had done its harm. Paul wrote to the

Corinthians, "For ye are yet carnal: for whereas there is among you envying, and strife, and divisions" (1 Corinthians 3:3). In the churches in Galatia the fellowship was fractured through the infiltration of the leaven of legalism. Paul stood firmly against the fake teaching, but he appealed to the Christians there to stand together and bear each other's burdens (Galatians 6:1-2).

The history of the Church is the record of a fractured fellowship. Disagreement in matters pertaining to doctrine, methods, behavioral standards, associations, and the like has created serious splits within the Body of Christ. Then too, as was pointed out earlier, unregenerated professors of religion have been accepted into the membership of many churches, so that in the outward visible church the progress of corruption and deterioration continues. The kingdom of Heaven in its outward manifestation in the age between the two advents of Christ will be marked by the subtle infiltration of a psuedo-Christianity which, while aping the outward form, denies the true essence and power. Even among evangelical groups today one does not find much of that true Biblical fellowship that is strengthened through Christians feeding on the "meal," namely, the Bible, God's written Word (Jeremiah 15:16), and the Lord Jesus Christ, the Incarnate Word (John 6:48-63).

That Woman

Finally, there is that woman whom our Lord mentioned in the parable. Does the woman represent good or evil? Those persons who believe she represents good are divided, some insisting she is the Church, others favor Israel. In the typology of Scripture a *woman* represents a religious system, sometimes for good and at other times for evil. The action of the woman in our Lord's parable is not good.

Notice that she *hid* the *leaven* in the meal. If the leaven represents that which is good, why hide it? "But if our gospel be hid, it is hid to them that are lost: In whom the god of this world hath blinded the minds of them which believe not, lest the light of the glorious gospel of Christ, who is the image of God, should shine unto them" (2 Corinthians 4:3-4). The gospel must be taken to all the world and to every person (Mark 16:15). Jesus commanded His disciples to preach it from the housetops (Matthew 10:27). The followers of our Lord did not sneak about deceitfully and dishonestly. They preached and witnessed openly. Paul and Peter and Jude wrote about those false teachers who crept in unawares with their heresies (Galatians 2:4; 2 Peter 2:1; Jude 4). Sneaking up on people with his false doctrine is Satan's way of working. The gospel of Christ is the power of God unto salvation, and of that gospel Paul said, "I am not ashamed" (Romans 1:16).

In the book of Revelation four significant women are mentioned. In chapters 2 and 3 our Lord sends a message to each of the seven churches in Asia. In His message to Thyatira, the fourth church, which corresponds to the fourth parable in Matthew 13, He said, "I have a few things against thee, because thou sufferest that woman Jezebel, which calleth herself a prophetess, to teach and to seduce My servants to commit fornication, and to eat things sacrificed unto idols'' (Revelation 2:20).

The Jezebel in Thyatira was a successor to the ancient Jezebel of Elijah's day. The wife of King Ahab, she had corrupted Israel through her prophets. They crept in among God's people introducing false doctrines and vile practices associated with the worship of Baal (1 Kings 17— 19; 21:25). Let us make no mistake about the woman in the parable of the leaven. She is doing no good thing.

With this fourth parable Jesus concluded His teaching in the presence of the multitude. All four parables are connected, portraying with consistency and continuity the course of the age between His two advents.

7

THE PARABLE OF THE HIDDEN TREASURE

Again, the kindgom of heaven is like unto treasure hid in a field; the which when a man hath found, he hideth, and for joy thereof goeth and selleth all that he hath, and buyeth that field (Matthew 13:44).

The last three parables in this series of seven form a group in themselves. After our Lord spoke the parable of the leaven, He dismissed the multitude and took His disciples into the house. Our chapter opened with the statement, "The same day went Jesus out of the house, and sat by the seaside. And great multitudes were gathered ... unto Him" (13:1-2). When He finished teaching the first four parables, He sent the multitude away and returned to the house with His disciples (13:36).

It is significant that these last three parables were given to the disciples only. The multitudes were mere casual hearers of what Christ taught; they were spectators only as He spoke those first four parables. Now, in the three remaining parables He will minister to those who truly and sincerely believe in Him. He will now reveal to His own what God is doing during that period between His first and second advents to earth. In the first four Satan is at work, but here the work of God is stressed.

There is a close similarity between the fifth and sixth parables, both having something in common. We will read them together so as to see how they are alike, and then study them as separate individual parables. "Again, the kingdom of heaven is like unto treasure hid in a field; the which when a man hath found, he hideth, and for joy thereof goeth and selleth all that he hath, and buyeth that field. Again, the kingdom of heaven is like unto a merchant man, seeking goodly pearls" (Matthew 13:44-45).

In both parables there is a man, in both he finds something he wants, and in both he sells all that he has to buy it. There are certain parts of these parables with which we are already familiar. First, there is "a field." There is no difficulty here because Jesus said, "The field is the world" (verse 38). Secondly, there is a man in the story. Again, there is no difficulty. The man is "the Son of man" (verse 37). There is a hidden treasure and a costly pearl that Christ wants. They are in the human race, in the world of humanity. What is this treasure and how does He acquire it?

Before we proceed to examine the Scriptures, I must say that I am opposed to one of the popular interpretations of these two parables which teaches that the treasure and the pearl represent salvation in Christ, or Christ Himself. The man in the parables is said to be the sinner who goes about seeking Christ. When he discovers Him, then he must sell all that he has, give it all up, and purchase Christ at any cost. But this whole idea is false. Christ is not hidden somewhere in the world, nor is He for sale. Moreover, it is not the sinner who seeks Christ. It is Christ who seeks the sinner. "For the Son of man is come to seek and to save that which was lost" (Luke 19:10). The sinner has nothing to offer Christ in exchange for salvation. Without Christ he is in a state of bankruptcy. Neither Christ nor salvation is the treasure in this parable.

What is the treasure? The answer is stated in the Bible. Three months after the children of Israel had left Egypt, and had come to the desert of Sinai, God gave this message to Moses, "Tell the children of Israel.... Now therefore, if ye will obey My voice indeed, and keep My covenant, then ye shall be a peculiar *treasure* unto Me above all people" (Exodus 19:3-5). The Psalmist wrote, "For the LORD hath chosen Jacob for Himself, and Israel for His peculiar *treasure*" (Psalm 135:4 RSV).

When God chose Israel to become His treasure, it was not because they were better than other nations. God wanted a people to represent Him, to be a repository for His Word, and to be an example of what a nation ought to be. God intended Israel to show to the rest of the world how any nation can be blessed with peace and prosperity through a right relationship to Himself. This was a great honor and privilege for Israel; however, it enjoined upon that nation a solemn responsibility. Israel was not to be God's treasure in name only, but a holy people before all the other nations of the world. Moses wrote, "For thou art an holy people unto the LORD thy God: the LORD thy God hath chosen thee to be a special people unto Himself, above all people that are upon the face of the earth. The LORD did not set His love upon you, nor choose you, because ye were more in number than any people; for ye were the fewest of all people: But because the LORD loved you, and because He would keep the oath which He had sworn unto your fathers, hath the LORD brought you out with a mighty hand, and redeemed you out of the house of bondmen, from the hand of Pharaoh king of Egypt'' (Deuteronomy 7:6-8). When God called Abraham He promised to bring forth a great nation and bless the people, and He added, ''and thou shalt be a blessing ... and in thee shall all families of the earth be blessed'' (Genesis 12:1-3). Israel was to be a witness to God's grace and power. She was to reflect His glory among all nations.

In this parable Israel is His treasure. However, when Christ came, Israel was no longer a shining example of what a people in fellowship with God should be. For more than seven hundred years Israel has been the military target of other nations. The people had violated God's laws and become involved in various forms of idolatry. As a result of their backsliding, God allowed them to suffer defeat at the hands of their enemies. When the Lord Jesus Christ appeared in His first advent, His treasure was hidden, that is, the people were scattered without a king. A remnant that returned from their latest captivity was then chafing under the bitter yoke of Rome. God's treasure had failed to fulfill her role.

The four hundred years between the two Testaments are often called ''the silent years'' because there was no contact between God and His treasure, not even a prophet to speak to the people for God. Where was the treasure? They were ''dispersed among the Gentiles'' (John 7:35). James wrote his Epistle ''to the twelve tribes which are scattered abroad'' (James 1:1). Peter likewise addressed his first Epistle ''to the strangers scattered throughout Pontus, Galatia, Cappadocia, Asia, and Bithynia'' (1 Peter 1:1). When the Son of man came to earth His treasure was "hid in a field," scattered throughout the known world. Israel as a nation was lost to the world as an influence for God.

When the Man came, the treasure was His first objective. John said, "He came unto His own" (John 1:11). When Jesus commissioned His twelve disciples He said, "Go not into the way of the Gentiles, and into any city of the Samaritans enter ye not: But go rather to the lost sheep of the house of Israel" (Matthew 10:5-6). He was seeking His treasure. After Pentecost Peter said to the Jews, "Unto you *first* God, having raised up His Son Jesus, sent Him to bless you, in turning away every one of you from his iniquities" (Acts 3:26). Even Paul was aware of the fact that Israel was God's treasure when he said to the Jews, "It was necessary that the Word of God should *first* have been spoken to you" (Acts 13:46). In his Epistle to the Romans the great apostle testified to his justifiable pride in the gospel because "it is the power of God unto salvation to every one that believeth; to the Jew *first*" (Romans 1:16). Israel, God's treasure, was the chief concern of the Lord Jesus Christ.

"He came unto His own." He found His treasure. But "His own received Him not" (John 1:11). They failed to recognize in Jesus their promised Messiah and Deliverer. As we saw earlier in our study, Israel's leaders rejected Him so He turned from them and hid the treasure again. The parable says, "The kingdom of heaven is like unto treasure hid in a field; the which when a man hath found, he hideth." He uncovered His treasure, but only for a brief period of time. When they said they would not have Him and openly rejected Him, He hid the treasure again.

As opposition mounted against our Lord, He withdrew from the nation, saying, "The kingdom of God shall be taken from you, and given to a nation bringing forth the fruits thereof" (Matthew 21:43). He was telling them that the privilege of showing forth the grace and glory of God would be taken from them, and that now they would go back into hiding.

But God will not leave Himself without a witness. If Israel, His treasure, refuses to obey Him, He will find another, a "pearl" who will become His mouthpiece during His absence from the earth. When Christ found His treasure, He was giving Israel another opportunity to appear as the leading nation among the other nations of the world, but Israel forfeited the opportunity.

Christ did not give up on Israel. After He found the treasure and hid it again, we read that "for joy thereof goeth and selleth all that He hath." I am pressing the point that He did not obtain the treasure until after He sold all that He had. The man who in His joy goes and sells all that He has is our Lord Jesus Christ. It was on the cross that He gave all—"Himself" (Galatians 2:20). "Who for the joy that was set before Him endured the cross, despising the shame, and is set down at the right hand of the throne of God" (Hebrews 12:2). What was the joy set before Him? It was the joy of knowing that in the Father's will He was paying the purchase price to redeem His treasure. What condescending love! He sold all that He had. "Who, being in the form of God, thought it not robbery to be equal with God: But made Himself of no reputation, and took upon Him the form of a servant, and was made in the likeness of men: And being found in fashion as a man, He humbled Himself, and became obedient unto death, even the death of the cross'' (Philippians 2:6-8). ''Forasmuch as ye know that ye were not redeemed with corruptible things, as silver and gold, from your vain conversation received by tradition from your fathers; But with the precious blood of Christ, as of a lamb without blemish and without spot'' (1 Peter 1:18-19). ''For ye know the grace of our Lord Jesus Christ, that, though He was rich, yet for your sakes, He became poor, that ye through His poverty might be rich'' (2 Corinthians 8:9). Yes, He gave all that He had.

The parable does not tell all the story about Israel's future. We do know that the treasure, though hidden today, will one day be in the control of its Creator and Redeemer. The future for Israel is bright with prospect. Israel is to be a witness to the world of the grace and power of her Messiah and Redeemer. The application of this parable goes beyond that first advent of Christ to the earth, looking ahead to His second advent.

Paul dealt with this subject fully in his Epistle to the Romans 9—11. These three chapters should be read at one sitting because in them one will find a detailed explanation of the parable of the hidden treasure: God's past selection of Israel (Romans 9); God's present suspension of Israel (Romans 10); God's prospective salvation of Israel (Romans 11).

These three chapters in Romans are a vital and an integral part of the Epistle and absolutely essential to its correct interpretation. In chapter 9 Paul is dealing with the past history of Israel as a nation. God, in His own sovereign will and purpose, selected this people as His treasure. Paul asks the question, "What shall we say then? Is there unrighteousness with God? God forbid" (9:14). Was God unjust in choosing one nation above others as His treasure? The answer is a resounding *No*. Perish the thought! Don't allow it even to enter your mind. There is never injustice in the choices of God. If we can't trust God in the matter of choosing and selecting, then whom can we trust? Because God chose Israel, envy, jealousy, and hatred have been aimed at the Jew. Many Gentiles do not approve of God's choice. But then, God being sovereign and righteous, never did submit His choice of Israel for a Gentile vote of confidence. Yes, Israel is God's treasure. Man must leave God to His sovereign righteous choices or else we must all perish.

In Romans 10 we learn why the treasure is hidden during this present dispensation. The chapter opens with a cry from Paul's heart in which he expresses the longing of his heart for Israel's salvation (verse 1). Their present situation, one in which God is not now dealing with the nation, is due to their own failure. Paul said, "They have a zeal of God, but not according to knowledge" (verse 2). Where did Israel fail? "For they being ignorant of God's righteousness, and going about to establish their own righteousness, have not submitted themselves unto the righteousness of God" (verse 3). They were not ignorant of the law, for they practically worshiped it. They were ignorant of the righteousness of God described in Romans 3:21, a righteousness which is apart from the law. Divine righteousness and human righteousness are mutually exclusive. Isaiah gave a fitting description of human righteousness when he said, "All our righteousnesses are as filthy rags'' (Isaiah 64:6). Paul had learned the difference between these two kinds of righteousness when he testified, ''Not having my own righteousness, which is of the law, but that which is through the faith of Christ, the righteousness which is of God by faith'' (Philippians 3:9). Self-righteousness erects a monument to the glory of man. God's righteousness, which is imputed to the sinner who trusts the finished work of Christ, glorifies God. ''But of Him are ye in Christ Jesus, who of God is made unto us wisdom, and righteousness, and sanctification, and redemption: That, according as it is written, He that glorieth, let him glory in the Lord'' (1 Corinthians 1:30-31). Jesus had warned the Jews, ''For I say unto you that except your righteousness shall exceed the righteousness of the scribes and Pharisees, ye shall in no case enter into the kingdom of heaven'' (Matthew 5:20). But they rejected Christ. Paul said, ''But they have not all obeyed the gospel'' (Romans 10:16). ''Christ is the end of the law for righteousness to every one that believeth'' (Romans 10:4), but Israel would not submit to Him. It was not because they *could not* believe in Him, but because they *would not*. And so, in this present dispensation there is no difference between the Jew and the Gentile (10:12). Both are on the same standing as sinners before God, salvation being offered to both on the same basis. Israel the treasure is hidden today in the sense that God is not now dealing exclusively with that nation.

In Romans 11 we have a clear presentation of God's future purpose for His treasure. A remnant will be regathered and redeemed as a nation. The treasure, though hidden, is not lost. God has not permanently rejected His people. All of the promises of God to Israel in the Old Testament will have a literal fulfillment. There are some theologians who have no place in their theological system for Israel's future salvation. But what do the Scriptures teach? "Hath God cast away His people? God forbid" (11:1). "God hath not cast away His people" (11:2). "Even so ... at this present time also there is a remnant according to the election of grace" (11:5). God still calls them "His people." "And so all Israel shall be saved: as it is written, There shall come out of Sion the Deliverer, and shall turn away ungodliness from Jacob: For this is My convenant unto them, when I shall take away their sins" (11:26-27). Presently Israel remains in a state of spiritual blindness, but her tragic state of affairs will not last forever. The present unbelief of the nation has not resulted in the canceling of God's ancient promises. Paul's point-blank denial that "God hath not cast away His people" has reference to Israel as a nation. The Old Testament prophets predicted the continuity of Israel as the treasure of Jehovah (Jeremiah 33:23-26). The same divine grace that saved Paul and many other Jews will function in the future to restore the treasure back into the favor of God. Here in Romans 11 the apostle is teaching that the present hardening of Israel against the Messiah is only temporary, "that blindness in part is happened to Israel, until the fullness of the Gentiles be come in" (11:25). And then "all Israel shall be saved" (11:26).

There is a striking similarity between the events in Romans 11 and the events outlined by Christ in Luke 21. In each passage there is a designated time period called "the times of the Gentiles" (Luke 21:24), or "the fullness of the Gentiles'' (Romans 11:25). This period is the present age during which God is visiting the Gentiles to take from among them a people for His Name (Acts 15:14). During this time Israel is in the background, the treasure being hidden. Then in each of the two passages, that time period closes with Israel being restored to the favor of God. In Luke we read of Israel's ''redemption'' when the Son of man comes with power and great glory (Luke 21:27-28). In Romans Paul says that Israel shall be ''saved'' when ''there shall come out of Sion the Deliverer, and shall turn away ungodliness from Jacob'' (Romans 11:26).

Even though Israel is presently the enemy of Christ and His gospel, that nation is still God's treasure, His elect nation. This is one of those ''mysteries of the kingdom'' given by our Lord in the parables recorded in Matthew 13, and of which Paul said, ''I would not, brethren, that ye should be ignorant of this mystery'' (Romans 11:25). God's gifts to Israel are not to be recalled (Romans 11:29). God made a promise to Abraham, Isaac, Jacob, and David, and God will never repent of those promises.

There is one pertinent thought in the parable calling for comment. It is in our Lord's statement that He ''buyeth that field'' (Matthew 13:44). Now we know that ''the field is the world'' (13:38). When Christ gave His all in sacrificial death at Calvary, He died for the whole world of mankind. The Scriptures place no limitation on the atoning death of Jesus Christ. The Apostle Paul said it was ''*unto all* and *upon all* them that believe: for there is no difference'' (Romans 3:22). Have you ever wondered why Paul said ''*unto* all and *upon* all''? *Unto all* means that the righteousness of God is universal, available to every person on earth. It is for everybody.

If it is *unto all*, then why aren't *all* saved? There is a condition involved. It is "*upon all* them that believe." Salvation is for all men if they want it, but it only rests upon those who believe in the Lord Jesus Christ. Peter wrote about the false prophets and false teachers, "who privily shall bring in damnable heresies, even denying the Lord that bought them, and bring upon themselves swift destruction" (2 Peter 2:1). Notice that they were part of "that field" that Christ bought. Their destruction they brought upon themselves. John wrote of our Lord that "He is the propitiation for our sins: and not for ours only, but also for the sins of the whole world" (1 John 2:2).

You are a part of that world whom God loves and for whom Christ died. When He gave His life on the cross to buy the field, you were included in the purchase. If you deny the Lord, then you bring upon yourself swift destruction. If you believe on the Lord Jesus Christ, God will both justify you and make you righteous.

Having seen that Christ bought the field, which is the world of humanity, we are now prepared to grasp the meaning of the next parable, the pearl of great price.

8

THE PARABLE OF THE PEARL

Again, the kingdom of heaven is like unto a merchant man, seeking goodly pearls: Who, when he had found one pearl of great price, went and sold all that he had, and bought it (Matthew 13:45-46).

As we study these parables we must keep fresh in our minds that all seven of them are dealing with activities during this present age between the two advents of our Lord Jesus Christ. In the first four parables we saw much of Satan's activity in his opposition to the Word and work of God. But in the parables of the hidden treasure and the pearl of great price, our Lord is showing us what He is doing in this present age. There is no mention of satanic activity.

In His first advent to the earth, our Lord came to His own people, the lost sheep of the house of Israel (Matthew 10:6; 15:24). They were His treasure, but they were hidden, "scattered abroad" (James 1:1), "strangers scattered throughout Pontus, Galatia, Cappadocia, Asia, and Bithynia" (1 Peter 1:1). He sought them out from their hiding places, presented Himself as their Messiah-King, and offered them the promised kingdom. But they rejected Him and His offer. He left them to their own choice and moved on to give Himself in sacrificial death, not merely for Israel, but for the whole world. He arose from death and the grave and ascended back to the throne in Heaven.

Now we must see how these two parables are linked together. They show us two aspects of the work of the cross. Christ died to redeem His treasure, Israel. But then there is another great treasure in the world that He values highly. He said, "And other sheep I have, which are not of this fold: them also I must bring, and they shall hear My voice; and there shall be one fold, and one shepherd" (John 10:16). It is what our Lord called the pearl of great price. The pearl, unlike the treasure, is not a Jewish stone. Many precious stones are named and described in the Old Testament, but the pearl is referred to only once: "No mention shall be made of coral, or of pearl" (Job 28:18). The pearl was a highly valued gem, and still is, in all parts of the world, but the Hebrews did not consider it of value. In the New Testament, pearls are mentioned not less than nine times, two of these occurring in this parable.

In order for us to understand the meaning of the parable, it is necessary that we know the meaning of the pearl. We learned from Scripture that the hidden treasure was Israel. But what does the pearl represent?

Such men as the good and gifted J.C. Ryle and C.H. Spurgeon believed that the hidden treasure and the pearl could not represent the sinner, but that they represented Christ. Bishop Ryle said, "These two parables are meant to teach us that men really convinced of the importance of salvation, will give up everything to win Christ and eternal life. The sinner sees in Christ an endless treasure and a precious pearl. To win Christ he will make any sacrifice. This is true faith." This view was so popular that someone expressed it in a hymn:

> I've found the Pearl of greatest price,
> My heart doth sing for joy;
> And sing I must, for Christ I have—
> Oh, what a Christ have I.

As we tried to show in our exposition of the parable of the hidden treasure, the above interpretation of these two parables is out of harmony with the total teaching of our Lord in all seven parables. What then did our Lord have in mind when He spoke the parable of the pearl of great price?

After Israel rejected Him, and before He gave His life for the world, Jesus used a term for the first time when He spoke of His *Church*. He said, "I will build My church, and the gates of hell shall not prevail against it" (Matthew 16:18). This was a truly great announcement coming from our Lord after His rejection by the Jews. I can see a remarkable parallelism in the teaching of Matthew 13 and 16. The events recorded in chapter 16 occurred only a short time after our Lord taught the parables of the kingdom. When Jesus asked the disciples if they understood *all* of His teaching of the parables, they answered, "Yea, Lord" (13:51). The truth of the matter is that they did not understand *all*. After our Lord's resurrection and just prior to His ascension they displayed their ignorance by asking, "Lord, wilt Thou at this time restore again the kingdom to Israel?" (Acts 1:6) Their timing was off, thereby showing they did not understand that there was to be the church age before Christ set up His kingdom on earth. They had not grasped the meaning of the parable of the pearl. Further teaching was needed on the subject of the Church.

In the parable of the hidden treasure, Israel is to go into hiding again and Christ will suffer and die. Through the shedding of His blood He will purchase the pearl. That pearl is the Church. When Jesus first spoke of His Church, it was not yet in existence, for when He said, ''I will build My church,'' He put it in the future tense—''I will build.'' The pearl was to be a product of His sufferings. ''Christ ... loved the church, and gave Himself for it'' (Ephesians 5:25). He ''sold all that He had, and bought it'' (Matthew 13:46).

In Paul's first Epistle to the Corinthians we read, ''Give none offence, neither to the Jews, nor to the Gentiles, nor to the church of God'' (1 Corinthians 10:32). This is God's way of describing in three terms the whole human race. Every person on earth is either an unsaved Jew, an unsaved Gentile, or a member of Christ's Church. By His death on the cross, Jesus broke down the wall of partition that separated Gentiles from Jews, ''that He might reconcile both unto God in one body by the cross'' (Ephesians 2:14-16). The ''one body'' is the Church (Ephesians 1:22-23; 4:4), the pearl of great price.

Christ made a tremendous statement about His Church. He said, ''The gates of hell shall not prevail against it.'' In the first four parables there was satanic opposition hindering both the Word and work of God. However, there is no force, however powerful, that can overcome Christ's Church. He gave Himself for it, ''that He might present it to Himself a glorious church, not having spot, or wrinkle, or any such thing; but that it should be holy and without blemish'' (Ephesians 5:27). This is His pearl, composed of all born-again Jews and Gentiles from Pentecost until Christ returns. The pearl is of inestimable worth to Him, described by Paul as "the riches of the glory of His inheritance in the saints" (Ephesians 1:18).

Let me suggest some possible reasons why Jesus might have chosen the pearl to symbolize the Church. We know that pearls are found inside of oysters. But how do they get there? Unlike other jewels and gems, the pearl is a product of life, the life of an oyster. No other precious stone is the product of a living organism. A grain of sand or some other foreign substance finds its way between the shells of the oyster. It is at once an irritant and becomes an annoyance to the oyster. In order to get relief, the oyster throws off a secretion which forms around the irritant. That secretion, called nacre, is best known as mother-of-pearl. It is the very life of the oyster. The process of surrounding the irritant with its secretion does not stop. The oyster continues to give of itself, growing weaker and weaker until it dies. It is through the suffering and death of the oyster that the pearl is perfected, an object of beauty. The offender, causing the death of the oyster, becomes a gem of great worth.

What a striking picture of the Church's formation! She is to the Merchantman that "one pearl of great price." The Merchantman is our Lord Jesus Christ, who came from Heaven to earth seeking the pearl. And what did He find? He found only unregenerate, unlovely, unworthy sinners. As the grain of sand tortured and grieved the oyster, even so the lost sinner Christ was seeking grieved His heart. Why would He ever want us? Why would He consider us to be of such "great price"? The Apostle Paul wrote,

"But God commendeth His love toward us, in that, while we were yet sinners, Christ died for us" (Romans 5:8). It was divine love that sent the Saviour in search of the sinner. Think of it! While we were sinning, God was proving and demonstrating His love for us. This is pure, unbounded, marvelous grace.

The pearl is produced by the suffering and death of the oyster. The suffering and death of our Lord Jesus Christ was the price He paid to produce His "pearl of great price." The parable says He "sold all that He had." The self-imposed poverty and suffering of our Saviour are indescribable. Paul said, "For ye know the grace of our Lord Jesus Christ, that, though He was rich, yet for your sakes He became poor, that ye through His poverty might be rich" (2 Corinthians 8:9). He was born in a borrowed manger, He preached from a borrowed boat, He rode on a borrowed beast, He was buried in a borrowed tomb. When a certain scribe said to Jesus that he would follow Him wherever He went, our Lord reminded him, "The foxes have holes, and the birds of the air have nests, but the Son of man hath not where to lay His head" (Matthew 8:19-20). Let us never forget that while "we were enemies, we were reconciled to God [through] the death of His Son" (Romans 5:10). The price was beyond all human computation, of which none of us are worthy. With His own precious blood He bought the whole world that He might find that pearl.

In all of this we must not fail to see the lowly origin of the pearl. It began as a grain of sand amidst mire and muck in the depths of the sea. In some Scriptures the sea is an acknowledged type of the restless Gentile nations. The

Prophet Isaiah wrote, "But the wicked are like the troubled sea, when it cannot rest, whose waters cast up mire and dirt" (Isaiah 57:20). In Daniel 7 we have the record of a vision Daniel saw, of which he said, "I saw in my vision by night, and, behold, the four winds of the heaven strove upon the great sea. And four great beasts came up from the sea" (Daniel 7:1-3). Those four beasts appearing from the sea represented four great Gentile world powers, the Babylonian, Medo-Persian, Greek, and Roman Empires. Jude saw them as "raging waves of the sea, foaming out their own shame" (Jude 13).

The pearl is never formed instantaneously. It is not produced in a day or a week or a month or a year. Layer upon layer of secretion, over a long period of time, produces the pearl. It is now more than nineteen hundred years since Jesus commenced building His Church. I have been in His Church for more than fifty years, and yet I have never seen that Church. Churches? Yes, I have seen many of them. As a matter of record, I have spoken in more than twelve hundred churches in America, and in my travels across the years I have witnessed new members being added to Christ's Church. And what a precious lot they are! I personally met some of them among the savage Auca Tribe in the jungles of South America, among the primitive Choco Indians in the jungles of Panama, among the Ifugao spear-carrying tribesmen in a northern province of the Philippines, and among both the rich and the poor in our own United States of America. And the work of completing the pearl continues, new members being added to the Church with each passing day. One of these days, and it could be soon, the pearl will be completed, and then the Lord Jesus Christ, who gave His all to purchase the Church, will come to take her to Himself, "a glorious church, not having spot, or wrinkle, or any such thing; but that it should be holy and without blemish" (Ephesians 5:27).

Another interesting feature of the pearl is its unity. Look again at our Lord's parable. "He ... found *one* pearl of great price." There are not many pearls, but *one* only. The Church is "*one* body" (Ephesians 4:4), "for ye are all *one* in Christ Jesus" (Galatians 3:28). Each member in the body is exhorted to guard that unity (Ephesians 4:3). It is possible to cut one diamond and divide it into several stones without depreciating its value; but not so the pearl. Once the pearl is broken it is destroyed. Using the body as a figure of speech, Paul describes the unity of the Church. He says, "For ... the body is *one*, and hath many members, and all the members of that *one* body, being many, are *one* body, so also is Christ. For by *one* Spirit are we all baptized into *one* body, whether we be Jews or Gentiles, whether we be bond or free; and have been all made to drink into *one* Spirit.... But now are they many members, yet but *one* body" (1 Corinthians 12:12-13,20).

Yes, beloved Christians, we are members of *one* body and Christ is our sovereign Head. Each of us must function under the direction of the Head, "for the edifying of the body of Christ: Till we all come in the unity of the faith, and of the knowledge of the Son of God, unto a perfect man, unto the measure of the stature of the fullness of Christ" (Ephesians 4:12-13).

Finally, there is the ultimate glory of the Church which awaits her completion. When Paul used the figure of a building to depict the Church, he said it "groweth unto an holy temple in the Lord" (Ephesians 2:21). When the last member is added to the body, and the last stone is added to the *building*, Christ will take it "to Himself a glorious church, not having spot, or wrinkle, or any such thing; but that it should be holy and without blemish" (Ephesians 5:27). Think of it! God is richer as the result of the pearl Jesus bought when He sold all that He had.

Have you ever wondered how God can be glorified in something of such lowly origin? Dr. Morgan said that it is a daring thought that God should gain something in us. Yet it is true that when Jesus gave all that He had to purchase the pearl, God was enriched. "He is enriched, not in essential glory, but by finding a medium through which that essential glory can be revealed." Paul said, "That in the ages to come He might show the exceeding riches of His grace in His kindness toward us through Christ Jesus" (Ephesians 2:7). The ultimate purpose of the Church is not her mission for a short time here on earth, but for eternity. The purpose of God in redeeming us was not merely our safety and happiness in Heaven, but His own glory. Through all eternity the whole of creation will see the trophy of His grace purchased through the sacrifice of His Son. The remembrance of God's goodness to us sinners will be hallowed throughout eternity.

In concluding our study of this parable, we should look at a statement from the pen of Peter. "Unto you therefore which believe He is precious" (1 Peter 2:7). For many years I read that passage interpreting it to mean that Christ is precious to the believer. Now it is absolutely true that He is precious (2:4). But that is not what Peter said in this verse. The Authorized Version does not present the literal rendering of the Greek text. What Peter did say was, ''Unto you that believe is the preciousness.'' In this verse the preciousness is *in* the believer. The Church, the pearl of great price, is a precious treasure to God. The moment we believed in the Lord Jesus Christ, His preciousness was communicated to us, and it is His preciousness in us on which God places a high value. And throughout eternity the pearl, His Church, will be the instrument through which God's love and grace and mercy will be displayed.

9

THE PARABLE OF THE NET AND FISHES

Again, the kingdom of heaven is like unto a net, that was cast into the sea, and gathered of every kind: Which, when it was full, they drew to shore, and sat down, and gathered the good into vessels, but cast the bad away. So shall it be at the end of the world: the angels shall come forth, and sever the wicked from among the just (Matthew 13:47-49).

We have come to the last parable in this series of seven. So as not to lose our perspective we will tie them all together, for in them our Lord is presenting in detail activities to occur during this present age. Keep in mind the fact that we are involved in those activities because we live in the unique period bounded by the two advents of Christ to the earth. The age of grace, or the church age, is included in that period.

Here is a prophetic panorama of the course of this age leading up to Christ's second coming to earth. The first four parables were spoken to the multitudes in the presence of the disciples. In them Jesus taught (1) that the age would be characterized by the sowing of the Word of God, but that there would not be a worldwide acceptance of the gospel; (2) Satan would do some sowing of his own, planting his children among the sons of God and imitating them; (3) the mixture of the counterfeit among the genuine produced the great mustard tree in whose

112

branches would be found the emissaries of Satan; (4) the professing church would be infiltrated by the leaven of false doctrine and foul deportment which would corrupt and disrupt the fellowship of God's people.

After relating these four parables, our Lord took His disciples into a house and gave to them privately the last three. The parable of the treasure hid in the field represents the nation of Israel whose future is bright at Christ's second coming. The parable of the pearl represents the Church, the redeemed company of Gentiles, with a minority of redeemed Jews, purchased by the sacrificial death of our Lord Jesus Christ. The third parable in this series of three, the *net and fishes*, will be the subject for our study in this chapter.

It will be helpful if we look again at 1 Corinthians 10:32: "Give none offence, neither to the Jews, nor to the Gentiles, nor to the church of God." These last three parables spoken to the disciples relate to the three classes of people, namely, the Jews, the Gentiles, and the Church. We saw that the parable of the hid treasure has to do with the Jew, and the pearl of great price represents the Church. Now we come to the final parable of the net and fishes. Only one group remains, the Gentile nations. The *net* in the parable is "cast into the sea" (Matthew 13:47), and the sea is used as a type of the nations. "The waters ... are peoples, and multitudes, and nations, and tongues" (Revelation 17:15).

Let us examine now this parable in the light of prophecy. The drawing of the net to shore takes place "at the end of the world" (Matthew 13:49), or, as the Greek text reads, "at the consummation of the age." The scene in the parable is one of judgment. This is not the judgment of those who are raised from the dead, but rather a judgment of the living nations, when Christ returns, to determine their relation to the kingdom. The Old Testament prophets predicted the drawing of the net when all nations would be gathered for that coming judgment:

> For, behold, in those days, and in that time, when I shall bring again the captivity of Judah and Jerusalem, I will also gather all nations, and will bring them down into the valley of Jehoshaphat, and will plead with them there for My people and for My heritage Israel, whom they have scattered among the nations, and parted My land (Joel 3:1-2).

> Assemble yourselves, and come, all ye heathen, and gather yourselves together round about: thither cause Thy mighty ones to come down, O LORD. Let the heathen be wakened, and come up to the valley of Jehoshaphat: for there will I sit to judge all the heathen round about (Joel 3:11-12).

> Therefore wait ye upon Me, saith the LORD, until the day that I rise up to the prey: for My determination is to gather the nations, that I may assemble the kingdoms, to pour upon them Mine indignation, even all My fierce anger: for all the earth shall be devoured with the fire of My jealousy (Zephaniah 3:8).

> For I will gather all nations against Jerusalem to battle; and the city shall be taken, and the houses rifled, and the women ravished; and half of the city shall go forth into captivity, and the residue of the people shall not be cut off from the city. Then shall the LORD go forth, and fight against those nations, as when He fought in the day of battle (Zechariah 14:2-3).

After reading these prophecies it is abundantly evident that all nations will be gathered for judgment at the end of the age. I believe this picture is more fully depicted in

Matthew 25:31-46, the parable of the net and the fishes being synonymous with our Lord's teaching in those verses. Here is a portion of the descriptive passage depicting the judgment of "all nations":

When the Son of man shall come in His glory, and all the holy angels with Him, then shall He sit upon the throne of His glory: And before Him shall be gathered all nations: and He shall separate them one from another, as a shepherd divideth his sheep from the goats: And He shall set the sheep on His right hand, but the goats on the left. Then shall the King say unto them on His right hand, Come, ye blessed of My Father, inherit the kingdom prepared for you from the foundation of the world: For I was an hungred, and ye gave Me meat: I was thirsty, and ye gave Me drink: I was a stranger, and ye took Me in: Naked, and ye clothed Me: I was sick, and ye visited Me: I was in prison, and ye came unto Me. Then shall the righteous answer Him, saying, Lord, when saw we Thee an hungred, and fed Thee? or thirsty, and gave Thee drink? When saw we Thee a stranger, and took Thee in? or naked, and clothed Thee? Or when saw we Thee sick, or in prison, and came unto Thee? And the King shall answer and say unto them, Verily I say unto you, Inasmuch as ye have done it unto one of the least of these My brethren, ye have done it unto Me. Then shall He say also unto them on the left hand, Depart from Me, ye cursed, into everlasting fire, prepared for the devil and his angels: For I was an hungred, and ye gave Me no meat: I was thirsty, and ye gave Me no drink: I was a stranger, and ye took Me not in; naked, and ye clothed Me not: sick, and in prison, and ye visited Me not. Then shall they also answer Him, saying, Lord, when saw we Thee an hungred, or athirst, or a stranger, or naked, or sick, or in prison, and did not minister unto Thee? Then shall He answer them, saying, Verily I say unto you, Inasmuch as ye did it not to one of the least of these, ye did it not to Me. And these shall go away into everlasting punishment: but the righteous into life eternal (Matthew 25:31-46).

The judgment scene in this passage will take place at the end of the tribulation and the beginning of Christ's millennial reign. After the Church has been "caught up" to meet the Lord in the air (1 Thessalonians 4:16-17), a remnant of Jewish believers will go forth preaching the gospel of the kingdom, announcing the coming of the King (Matthew 24:14). The Gentile nations will have one more opportunity to hear the good news of the gospel and the coming of the Messiah. The message they will hear, namely, "the gospel of the kingdom," will be the same message preached by John the Baptist, Jesus, and His disciples. But when the Jews rejected their King, the kingdom was postponed and the message discontinued. However, just prior to the King's second coming the message will be heralded again. God will seal 144,000 saved Jews to be the empowered messengers of the coming of the King and His kingdom.

Some will receive the message and be saved, "a great multitude, which no man could number, of all nations" (Revelation 7:9). Others will reject the message and persecute the Lord's messengers. Those who become saved will enter the kingdom and inherit its blessings. Those who rejected the message and persecuted the Jewish witnesses "shall [be] cast ... into the furnace of fire: there shall be wailing and gnashing of teeth" (Matthew 13:50). Their judgment I understand to be the separation of the tares from the wheat, and the bad fish from the good at "the end of the age."

The good fish of the parable will be blessed with an abundant portion in the coming kingdom. "Then shall the King say unto them on His right hand, Come, ye blessed of My Father, inherit the kingdom prepared for you from the foundation of the world" (Matthew 25:34). The prophet wrote of them, For "every one that is left of all the nations which came against Jerusalem shall even go up from year to year to worship the King, the LORD of hosts, and to keep the feast of tabernacles" (Zechariah 14:16). "Then shall the righteous shine forth as the sun in the kingdom of their Father" (Matthew 13:43). Yes, the King and His kingdom will come, and many will share the blessings of that golden age.

What are some practical lessons we may learn from this seventh parable? First, there is a solemn warning to all who hear the Word of God. The great net sweeping through the sea of nations, as I see it, is the gospel message. Many people are in the net. All of them have heard the truth of the gospel; however, the response has not been the same in every case. In Christendom there are the tares among the wheat, and bad fish mingling with the good. Obviously the bad did not deal honestly with the truth they heard. They did not totally reject it, but neither did they totally surrender to the Christ of the gospel. Many professing believers are in the net to whom our Lord referred as "the wicked" (13:49).

When any person hears the truth of the gospel, he has arrived at a point in his experience where he must make a decision. If he believes the truth and sincerely acts upon it, he is born again, he becomes a new creation, and he is never the same person again. If he merely professes to believe it, and goes on playing the hypocrite, the day of judgment will come. When the net is brought to shore at the end of the age, he will be exposed for the bad fish that he is. This seventh parable is tied closely to the first in which Christ warned us all, "Who hath ears to hear, let him hear" (Matthew 13:9). "Take heed therefore how ye hear" (Luke 8:18). It is dangerous business to be exposed to divine truth, to profess faith in it, and refuse to obey it. That is the first lesson we all must learn from this parable. Judgment is waiting at the end of the age.

The second lesson we Christians can learn from this seventh parable is suggested in our Lord's use of the plural pronoun *they*. Speaking of the net He said, "When it was full, *they* drew it to shore" (Matthew 13:48). He doesn't tell us who *they* are; however, it appears that human hands are assisting in gathering in the fish. Our Lord does not do His work alone. He said to His disciples, "Follow Me, and I will make you fishers of men" (Matthew 4:19). In Luke's account of the great catch of fishes, Jesus said, "From henceforth thou shalt catch men" (Luke 5:10). Even in the performing of His miracles Jesus sometimes used men, as when He fed the multitude (Matthew 15:32-39), and turned the water into wine (John 2:1-8). *They* who drew the net in the parable are not named. Moreover, the word "they" appears only once in the parable. The servants are in the background like John, who said of our Lord, "He must increase, but I must decrease" (John 3:30). When hero worship crept into the church at Corinth, Paul reminded the saints there that the minister is *nothing*. He is merely a vessel in God's hands, and that God Himself, and He only can give the increase (1 Corinthians 3:1-7). We who serve the Lord need to be reminded that we are mere instruments, and that God can dispense with any of us and carry out His program. Let us ply the sea with the gospel net, and at the same time remain in the background, "that in all things He might have the preeminence" (Colossians 1:18).

A third lesson we may learn from this parable is the obvious need for the gospel among all men. The gospel net must spread over the entire world. Jesus said to His disciples, "Go ye into all the world, and preach the gospel to every creature" (Mark 16:15). The whole inhabited earth must hear the gospel, and it will. The task will be completed during the tribulation, before our Lord returns to earth. He gave assurance of it when He said, "And this gospel of the kingdom shall be preached in all the world for a witness unto all nations; and then shall the end come" (Matthew 24:14). "The end" in this passage is the end of the tribulation when Christ returns. We Christians of this present dispensation have both the privilege and responsibility of helping spread the good news of Christ's gospel. It appears that we might be approaching the end, that the rapture of the Church might be very near. Top priority in the mind of every child of God should be a willingness to share the good news of salvation with those who are yet unsaved.

The fourth lesson we can learn from this seventh parable is a reiteration of what Jesus taught in the first four parables, namely, the bad will be mingled with the good. The desire of the fishermen in casting the net was to catch *good* fish. But when they drew the net to shore they discovered *bad* fish in the net. As we spread the gospel and reach all men with its message, we must not expect that all who profess to receive the Lord Jesus Christ will be truly born again. The tares will appear among the wheat.

Buzzards will appear in the branches of Christendom.

Now we may not be responsible for the *bad* fish in the net, but we should distinguish between the *good* and the *bad*. I see in this parable the principle of separation. The Apostle Paul wrote, "Now I beseech you, brethren, mark them which cause divisions and offences contrary to the doctrine which ye have learned; and avoid them" (Romans 16:17). "And have no fellowship with the unfruitful works of darkness, but rather reprove them" (Ephesians 5:11). We are not to play the role of moral detectives spying out the sins of our fellow men. But we must "Prove [or test] all things; hold fast that which is good" (1 Thessalonians 5:21). When positive action is called for, we have only to obey the plain teaching of Scripture which says, "Wherefore come out from among them, and be ye separate, saith the Lord, and touch not the unclean thing; and I will receive you" (2 Corinthians 6:17).

Now that we have drawn some practical lessons from this seventh parable, I feel an urgency to present a few words as to its primary interpretation. The judgment scene in verses Matthew 13:39-40,49-50 takes place at the end of the tribulation. The rapture (catching away) of the pearl (the Church) does not occur at "the end of the age" mentioned in verses 39 and 49. Angels are associated with the judgment at *the end of the age*, but angels are never said to be a separating influence when Christ comes for His Church. At the rapture the Church is separated from the unbelievers by the Lord Himself (1 Thessalonians 4:16-17), not by angels. The rapture separates the believer from the unbeliever; the return of Christ to earth with His angels after the tribulation separates the wicked from those who are saved during the tribulation.

We who are the redeemed of this present dispensation are never told to look for signs, nor a worldwide conversion of sinners, nor antichrist, nor angels, but for the appearing of our Lord Jesus Christ. ''Looking for that blessed hope, and the glorious appearing of the great God and our Saviour Jesus Christ'' (Titus 2:13). His appearing to gather His redeemed to Himself is the next event in God's prophetic program.

10

THE POSTSCRIPT

So shall it be at the end of the world: the angels shall come forth, and sever the wicked from among the just, And shall cast them into the furnace of fire: there shall be wailing and gnashing of teeth. Jesus saith unto them, Have ye understood all these things? They say unto Him, Yea, Lord. Then said He unto them, Therefore every scribe which is instructed unto the kingdom of heaven is like unto a man that is an householder, which bringeth forth out of his treasure things new and old (Matthew 13:49-52).

The late Bishop Ryle used to say, ''Personal application is the soul of preaching. A sermon without application is like a letter posted without a name or an address on the envelope. The letter may be well written, rightly dated, and properly signed. But it is useless, because it never reaches its destination.''

Our Lord concluded this series of parables with the searching question, ''Have ye understood all these things?'' (Matthew 13:51) The mere hearing of the parables would profit the hearers nothing. If the message is to produce the desired results, both the intellect and conscience must respond. The Apostle James wrote, ''But be ye doers of the Word, and not hearers only, deceiving your own selves'' (James 1:22). If every church member were examined at the end of the year as to how much Biblical knowledge he has learned and understood and put into practice, many of them would be found as ignorant as the heathen who never heard a message from God's Word.

The verses before us are a necessary part of this parable. They should challenge our thinking and search our hearts. No individual is born into this world and grows up a possessor of divine truth. "There is none that understandeth, there is none that seeketh after God" (Romans 3:11). But when any person, saved or unsaved, hears the truth of God's Word, he is responsible to God for his response to that truth. Willful ignorance is inexcusable. The Apostle Paul wrote about those persons who "did not like to retain God in their knowledge," therefore "God gave them over to a reprobate mind, to do those things which are not convenient" (Romans 1:28). We must answer to God for the knowable as well as for the known. (See 2 Peter 3:5.) When a person hears the truth of God, believes it, and acts in obedience upon it, he will never be the same again. We can see and understand now why Jesus said, "Have ye understood all these things?"

The hearing of the Word of God demands a choice. Wherever, whenever, and to whomsoever the Word of God is preached, the hearer is faced with the greatest and most important decision of life. Ever since our Lord spoke these parables, the seed of God's Word has been sown and continues to be sown, and the hearers have been making choices. Some, like King Agrippa in Paul's day and the Jews in Christ's time, made the wrong choice. But when the age draws to a close there will be the dividing of the good from the bad. Those who made the right choice will enter into Christ's kingdom. Those who rejected the truth, ''shall [be] cast ... into the furnace of fire: there shall be wailing and gnashing of teeth.''

But when our Lord asked, ''Have ye understood all these things?'' He was speaking to those disciples who had already believed in Him. They answered, ''Yea, Lord.'' As was pointed out earlier, later events proved that they had not grasped the full significance of what He had taught. But taking them at their word He immediately launched into an application directed to them. He commenced with the word ''therefore.'' They said they understood His teaching in the parables, therefore a new responsibility is enjoined upon them. ''Therefore every scribe which is instructed unto the kingdom of heaven is like unto a man that is an householder, which bringeth forth out of his treasure things new and old'' (Matthew 13:52).

This statement by Christ in verse 52 has been identified by some ministers of God's Word as the eighth parable in the chapter. I will not argue the point lest, while majoring on minors, we miss the thrust of what He said. Israel did not understand because they chose not to understand (13:10-16). The disciples were at least good hearers and willing learners. Now the Teacher will expect response from His pupils.

The responsibility of the learner is to instruct others. Daniel wrote, ''And they that understand among the people shall instruct many'' (Daniel 11:33). Hearing the Word and having a heart acquaintance with it is a precious privilege, but the one who has God's truth is like a ''householder,'' a house owner, the authoritative head of the house. The Greek word is *oikodespotes*. It occurs twelve times in the New Testament and is used only by

Jesus. Everyone of Christ's true followers is like a man who is the head of a house. In that home there are things of value, some new and some old. Jesus calls them a "treasure." What the home owner does with that treasure is important.

With almost monotonous regularity I have been reminding all of us that these parables set forth the prophecies and history of the kingdom between the two advents of the King. We are living in that period of time. Those of us who have been born again into the kingdom, and have been discipled in the truth Jesus taught, have a responsibility during that period of time. We have studied our Lord's parables and His explanation of the first two of them.

Now He asks us, do you *understand* them? Dr. Morgan has pointed out that the word translated "understood" means quite literally "to put together." Our Lord had taught them in the parables what could be expected during His absence and until He returns. What He asks is whether they can put together *all* those things. Did they see the whole picture as He presented it to them? If they did, they were to do what the scribes did under the old covenant, namely, interpret God's laws. In order for the disciples to carry out their mission they had to be the messengers of the old law as well as the new truths Christ had just taught them in the parables. If they could discern between the old and the new, if they could put the two together in proper perspective, they were obligated to bring them forth to others.

The truth Jesus taught He calls a treasure. The whole of the Word of God, both Old and New Testaments, is a veritable treasure indeed. But it must be understood and explained in the light of Christ's teaching in these parables. If we are householders and true to our calling, then we must present the truth without apology. What treasure we have for this age! And of that treasure we are stewards, custodians, caretakers. What are we to do with it? We must share the treasure bountifully with others.

In the first parable the age commenced with the sowing of the seed of God's Word, and that is to continue to the end of the age. The age will be one of conflict and the counterfeit. Both interference with the gospel and imitation of it must be expected. But we have vast resources. Let us scatter them, and in so doing let us not become discouraged if great numbers do not respond favorably. The parables have explained the course of the age. Our business is to bring forth the treasures of God's Word. This is God's purpose for His own. On the human side we see a deterioration in society as the age runs its course. But we see also the age from God's viewpoint.

As we look back upon history we can see how the shape of events is exactly as our Lord predicted in the parables. And those parables are the key to the future until Christ returns. So, "Let us not be weary in well doing: for in due season we shall reap, if we faint not" (Galatians 6:9). Neither man nor Satan can frustrate the plans of God. "Therefore, my beloved brethren, be ye stedfast, unmoveable, always abounding in the work of the Lord, forasmuch as ye know that your labour is not in vain in the Lord" (1 Corinthians 15:58).

PART TWO

THE LETTERS IN REVELATION 2—3

11

THE MYSTERY OF THE SEVEN CHURCHES

Write the things which thou hast seen, and the things which are, and the things which shall be hereafter; The mystery of the seven stars which thou sawest in My right hand, and the seven golden candlesticks. The seven stars are the angels of the seven churches: and the seven candlesticks which thou sawest are the seven churches (Revelation 1:19-20).

As Genesis is the book of *beginnings*, so Revelation is the book of *endings*. The book of Revelation is as necessary to the completion of the Bible as the head is to the body. It adds the finishing touches to the full-length portrait which the Bible gives of our Lord and the preparation of the earth for His second coming. This last book in the Bible is both a revelation of Jesus Christ and a revelation *from* Jesus Christ. Here we see the unveiling of His *Person* and His future *program*.

The book commences and concludes with a promised blessing to those persons who read and heed its message. "*Blessed* is he that readeth, and they that hear the words of this prophecy, and keep those things which are written therein: for the time is at hand" (Revelation 1:3). "Behold, I come quickly: *blessed* is he that keepeth the sayings of the prophecy of this book" (Revelation 22:7). No other book in the Bible is so heartily commended to its readers, and only here is that special blessing pronounced.

Ministers of God's Word will do well to heed this fact, and the recognition of it may result in a blessing which will surprise both themselves and their congregations.

The Apostle John wrote, "And he saith unto me, Seal not the sayings of the prophecy of this book: for the time is at hand" (Revelation 22:10). These words had a local and an immediate direction when they were first written; however, there is a deeper and wider significance. The message of the book of Revelation is not a sealed book but an open one, and meant to be kept so till the end.

No less than five times we find the expression, "the words" or "the sayings of the prophecy of this book" (1:3; 22:7,10,18-19). Here is an illustration of the law of recurrence. Such repetition suggests truth of unusual importance and compels our most careful and thoughtful attention. This law of recurrence gives emphasis to a truth that supplies a key to the interpretation of the book. The message cannot be understood until it is read in the light of this phrase. When the book was first written the whole of its contents, excepting the first chapter, had reference to the future.

Here the veil is drawn aside and we are presented with a succession of panoramic visions which John saw. One interesting feature is that the rays of God's lamp of prophecy are turned first upon the church (1:4). After the first chapter, which is introductory, our Lord sends a message to the churches. He said to John, "I am Alpha and Omega, the first and the last: and, What thou seest, write in a book, and send it unto the seven churches which are in Asia; unto Ephesus, and unto Smyrna, and unto Pergamos, and unto Thyatira, and unto Sardis, and unto

Philadelphia, and unto Laodicea" (Revelation 1:11). The messages in chapters 2 and 3 were addressed to seven churches then existing in Asia. However, they are typical and prophetic of the history of Christian profession throughout the entire church age.

After our Lord told John to write to the seven churches, John turned to the area from which the voice came. He wrote, "And being turned, I saw seven golden candlesticks [or, lampstands]" (1:12). We are not left in any uncertainty concerning the interpretation of the symbol, for John was told that "the seven candlesticks which thou sawest are the seven churches" (1:20). We see then that the Revelation is addressed locally to seven churches in Asia, but it is not limited and confined to them. Their purpose and application are much wider.

Now, we know that there were other churches existing at that time beside these seven. For instance, there were churches in Corinth, Galatia, Philippi, Colosse, Thessalonica, and many more. We are not told why Christ chose the seven churches in Asia. We do know that *seven* is the numeral which represents divine completeness. The application of the messages was never intended to be limited to those seven local assemblies. Each of the seven epistles closes with the exhortation, "He that hath an ear, let him hear what the Spirit saith unto the churches" (2:7,11,17,29; 3:6,13,22). It is not what the Spirit is saying merely to those seven churches; all churches are included in these messages. The entire Christian profession is in view.

At this point in our study I present a page from my commentary on Revelation:

The messages to the churches have a threefold meaning. First, each letter has a *primary association*, having a local and direct bearing upon the church to which it was written. We must not fail to see this. Certainly the letters were intended to be meaningful and helpful to those Christians in each church who first received the message. Each letter was a measuring rod by which each church could know its standing in the sight of the risen Lord.

Secondly, each letter has a *personal application*. In addition to being historical and local as regards an assembly in each city named, the message to each applies to every individual Christian. To each church Christ says, "*He* that hath an ear, let *him* hear what the Spirit saith unto the churches" (2:7,11,17,29; 3:6,13,22). It should also be noted that even though Christ addresses each church *as a whole*, the message to overcome is addressed to the individual (2:7,11,17,26; 3:5,12,21).

Thirdly, each church individually, and the seven churches combined, set forth *prophetic anticipation*. I see in them seven ages or stages in the life of *the* Church on earth, commencing with Pentecost and concluding with the Rapture.... When John wrote he probably did not see that each epistle contained an announcement of the future, any more than did David when he wrote Psalm 22. Nevertheless there is a prophetic picture of seven periods of the Church's history on earth. For myself, I do not doubt for one moment that a prophetic foreview of the entire Church dispensation was in the mind of our Lord when He dictated the letters to John. My personal study of church history brings me to this conclusion.[1]

I am not stating that the entire Church on earth would homogeneously pass from one stage to the other. Rather, that during this entire interadvent period, somewhere on earth there would be found the dominant characteristics of

[1]Lehman Strauss, *The Book of the Revelation*, pages 33-34.

the seven churches of the Revelation. Those characteristics would rise in church history successively within the professing church. As we look back upon nineteen hundred years of church history, there seems to be an amazing correspondence between the details mentioned concerning the seven churches in Asia and the successive periods of ecclesiastical history. The dominant characteristics of the seven Asian congregations do appear to have risen in church history successively and in the order given in Revelation 2—3. It seems almost incredible that such a progression should be accidental or incidental. However, it is only fair to add that the prophetic interpretation of the messages to the seven churches is not stated explicitly in the passage itself, but it is fully in keeping with the futurist approach to the book of Revelation.

If at this point I appear repetitious it is only because I sense the need to press and impress upon my reader the fact that these churches are no mere fiction, but historical churches. They actually existed. They were chosen because together they constitute a picture of the entire Church in the world at any place and at any time during the present dispensation. Therefore, these messages concern us as directly as they concerned the churches to which they were originally sent.

We propose to show that there is a striking correspondency between the seven messages addressed to the seven churches and the seven parables in Matthew 13. When the parallelisms between the two are brought together we see seven complete pictures which view the entire history of Christian profession from its beginning until Christ returns. These prophetic pictures parallel the changing conditions in the Church down through the centuries. I doubt that the Christians who lived during the early centuries of church history could see this parallel. But as we look back into history we are able to identify the period in which we are now living. There are secrets unfolded in these seven letters which present the true picture of church history.

As the student reads through Revelation 2—3 he will notice that the Lord commends each church for the good He sees in it and rebukes each for the wrong He finds. In not one of the churches did the Word preached produce a hundred per cent in good fruit. The Lord's criticism of the sins and weaknesses in those churches reveals the same conditions He taught in the seven parables. In each church can be found the wheat and the tares, the leaven, the good and bad fish. Here we find again, as we saw in the parables, a prophetic preview of church history. I believe this to be one of the reasons why Jesus chose these particular churches and placed them in this order. In these seven typical churches we have a picture of the predominant characteristics of seven successive eras of ecclesiastical history.

A fact not to be overlooked is our Lord's use of the word "mystery" in reference to the seven parables and the seven churches. We have already commented on Matthew 13:11, where Christ speaks of "the *mysteries* of the kingdom of heaven." In Revelation 1:20 He has John writing the following: "The *mystery* of the seven stars which thou sawest in My right hand, and the seven golden candlesticks. The seven stars are the angels of the seven churches: and the seven candlesticks which thou sawest are the seven churches." It is no mere incident that in these two passages Jesus uses the term "mystery."

In Matthew 13 He spoke seven parables which reveal the history of the kingdom of Heaven including Christendom, the external or outward view of the Church as man sees her. In Revelation 2—3 He dictated seven letters in which He revealed secrets of the Church, the internal view as God sees her. Both *mysteries* include the Church and the same time period. The mysteries were meaningless to the outsiders who did not possess the key but meaningful now to the believer who does have the key. The inner meaning is made plain. In Revelation 1:20 our Lord is preparing the reader for the unveiling of a *secret*. He is about to lead us on a journey through church history.

One key verse (1:19) divides the entire book into three periods of time—past, present, and future.

"*The things which thou hast seen.*" The things John saw refer to the vision of Christ as recorded in chapter 1. This portrait of the eternal and glorified Christ we should read often. He is portrayed here as in no other single chapter in the Bible. He is the main Subject of the entire book.

"*The things which are.*" These are the things which belong to the same era and dispensation to which John belonged and to which we belong. John lived and wrote in the dispensation of grace, of the Holy Spirit and the preaching of the gospel. John belonged to the church age just as we belong to the church age. "*The things which are*" constitute the burden of this section in our present study. They make up the history of the Church prewritten from Pentecost to the rapture and recorded in chapters 2—3.

"*The things which shall be hereafter.*" These "things" are future and they comprise chapters 4—22. Chapter 4 begins with the words, "Come up hither, and I will shew thee things which must be hereafter" (4:1). Everything in the book from chapter four to the end has to do with prophecies to be fulfilled after the Church is removed from the earth, after our Lord has taken His pearl of great price to Himself. After chapter 3 the Church is never mentioned again because she is not on the earth during that time period discussed in chapters 4—22.

These three divisions are clear, and it is the only outline in the context which allows the book to speak for itself. It is this outline which establishes a futuristic approach to the book of the Revelation. If the student will hold fast to this outline he will not be led astray nor become confused. Revelation 1:19 is the key to the book.

From this point on we will examine briefly "*the things which are,*" the secrets of church history revealed in the seven letters to the seven churches in chapters 2—3.[1]

[1]For a detailed discussion of the seven letters see the author's, *The Book of the Revelation*, pages 33-124.

12

THE LETTER TO EPHESUS

LABOR WITHOUT LOVE

Unto the angel of the church of Ephesus write; These things saith He that holdeth the seven stars in His right hand, who walketh in the midst of the seven golden candlesticks; I know thy works, and thy labour, and thy patience, and how thou canst not bear them which are evil: and thou hast tried them which say they are apostles, and are not, and hast found them liars: And hast borne, and hast patience, and for My name's sake hast laboured, and hast not fainted. Nevertheless I have somewhat against thee, because thou hast left thy first love. Remember therefore from whence thou art fallen, and repent, and do the first works; or else I will come unto thee quickly, and will remove thy candlestick out of his place, except thou repent. But this thou hast, that thou hatest the deeds of the Nicolaitans, which I also hate. He that hath an ear, let him hear what the Spirit saith unto the churches; To him that overcometh will I give to eat of the tree of life, which is in the midst of the paradise of God (Revelation 2:1-7).

At the time this message was addressed to the church at Ephesus, the city was an important and imposing one. It was the leading city in Asia Minor, prosperous in its commercial life, powerful in its political life, and popular for its learning and art. It was tremendously religious but the religion was heathen and idolatrous. For people entering Asia, Ephesus was inevitably the gateway to that continent.

Ephesus was the Vatican of its day, not papal of course, but pagan nevertheless. It was the center of the worship of Artemis, called "Diana of the Ephesians" (Acts 19:28). The temple built in honor to that goddess was one of the seven wonders of the ancient world. We have only to read Luke's full account in Acts 19 to see how much the goddess and her temple meant to the people in Ephesus. No city in Asia held less promise for sowing the seed of the gospel of Christ.

Yet it was in Ephesus where Christianity had some of its greatest triumphs. It was through the efforts of the fearless Apostle Paul that there occurred a complete turnabout in that city. Paul remained in Ephesus longer than in any other city, preaching the Word of God there for about three years (Acts 20:31). If anyone had doubts about the Word of God being "quick, and powerful, and sharper than any twoedged sword" (Hebrews 4:12), those doubts would have vanished at Ephesus. In Paul's day there could have been no other place which more effectively proved the conquering power of the Christian message. One needs only to read Acts 19—20 to see some of the fruits of Paul's labors in that city.

It was some thirty years later that John recorded our Lord's messages to the seven churches, the letter to the Ephesians being the first of the seven. The first vision in the book of Revelation, that of the exalted Christ in relation to, and walking in the midst of the churches, is the main vision in the entire book. The total vision takes in the first three chapters. After that magnificent portrait of Christ in chapter one there follows a further description of Him in chapters 2—3. Each of the seven letters begins with a descriptive term or group of terms setting forth one or more aspects of Christ's Person and work. It will not serve our purpose here to dwell upon those Scriptures, inasmuch as this study is intended to show some prophetic parallels between the seven parables in Matthew 13 and the seven letters in Revelation 2—3.

In each of the seven letters our Lord said, "*I know thy works*" (2:2,9,13,19; 3:1,8,15). He, being the omniscient One, sees and knows all things, therefore He is qualified to commend or criticize. He commenced with a word of commendation. Now we know that the church at Ephesus was at one time one of the strongest and most flourishing churches of all. Paul laid the foundation and Timothy followed and built upon that foundation. Then the Apostle John, who penned the seven letters, had labored about two years among the believers there. The church at Ephesus had a good start.

It Was Sound in Doctrine

We know the church at Ephesus was sound in doctrine from the description the Lord Himself gives of her. He said, "Thou hast tried them which say they are apostles, and are not, and hast found them liars" (2:2). The Christians at the Ephesian assembly knew what they believed and why they believed it. They had been taught the truth of God, and upon that truth they stood firmly. Rooted and grounded in the truth, they could not be moved.

Before Paul departed from Ephesus he warned the elders that false apostles with erroneous teaching would come among them. He said, ''Take heed therefore unto yourselves, and to all the flock, over the which the Holy Ghost hath made you overseers, to feed the church of God, which He hath purchased with His own blood. For I know this, that after my departing shall grievous wolves enter in among you, not sparing the flock. Also of your own selves shall men arise, speaking perverse things, to draw away disciples after them'' (Acts 20:28-30). The implication is that the problem was a matter of doctrine, and those Christians were able to distinguish clearly between the teaching of Christ's true apostles and Satan's false apostles. Evidently men had appeared in their midst who called themselves apostles of Christ and defended the right to this title. But the believers had been correctly indoctrinated and could not be deceived.

Now there is a church for you! What a wonderful church it was! Any Christian moving to Ephesus would have sought out that assembly and have felt proud to become a part of the fellowship. And why not? There aren't many churches in which the leaders are soundly indoctrinated Biblically. After all, Satan's counterfeit is a clever imitation of the authentic. Paul said, ''For such are false apostles, deceitful workers, transforming themselves into the apostles of Christ'' (2 Corinthians 11:13). It takes a man of the Word who is spiritually minded to detect false doctrine.

The parallel between the parables in Matthew 13 and this first letter to Ephesus is obvious. In the first parable the pure unadulterated Word was being sown. But the enemy was busy warring against the pure doctrines of the Word, and he continues to sow his tares among the wheat, an aggressive activity that will continue throughout this dispensation to its very end. In one of his later Epistles Paul wrote, "Now the Spirit speaketh expressly, that in the latter times some shall depart from the faith, giving heed to seducing spirits, and doctrines of devils" (1 Timothy 4:1). The Church has always been invaded by teachings "contrary to sound doctrine" (1 Timothy 1:10). But the church at Ephesus "continued stedfastly in the apostles' doctrine" (Acts 2:42). No doubt there were elders there who were worthy of double honor, especially those "who labour in the Word and doctrine" (1 Timothy 5:17). How otherwise could they have exposed and expelled the false apostles? The best defense against false doctrines is a thorough knowledge and a forthright declaration of the pure doctrines of the Bible. Doctrinally the church at Ephesus was sound.

It Was Strict in Discipline

Sound doctrine is usually connected with strict discipline. Where the one is present usually the other is to be found. The word *doctrine* means *teaching*. One of the main reasons why so many churches of today are in such a weak and miserable condition is the absence of doctrine and discipline. In any church where the Bible is not taught in a consistent, consecutive, and constructive manner, that church is miserably weak and wanting.

Now the letter does not say in so many words that the church in Ephesus tried these false apostles officially and then excommunicated them from the church. But it does say to them in the church, "how thou canst not bear them

which are evil" (2:2). The false teachers and evil workers
were not tolerated in that congregation. If they persisted
in their attempts to peddle their poison, then they were
not welcome. Mind you, these were not "tares" that were
not distinguishable from "wheat." The elders at Ephesus
had "tried them ... and ... found them liars."

The exercise of discipline was one of the strong points in
the earlier days of the Christian Church. In Samaria, when
the Holy Spirit brought forth a revival under the ministry
of Philip, an imposter named Simon appeared. He
professed to be a believer even to the extent of being
baptized (Acts 8:5-13). But he never had been converted.
God used Peter to discern the matter and discipline the
man (8:17-23). Ananias and Sapphira were severely
chastised for their sin (Acts 5:1-11). In the church at
Corinth a fornicator was sternly censured for his bad
behavior (1 Corinthians 5:1-5).

The question is sometimes asked, Why does God allow
such intrusion of evil into His Church? In both the
parables and the seven letters this is one of the
"mysteries." When Paul wrote Second Thessalonians he
said, "For the *mystery* of iniquity doth already work"
(2:7). It is no longer a mystery (or secret) that iniquity will
abound. When our Lord gave to His disciples some signs
of the end of the age and His second advent to earth He
said, "Iniquity shall abound" (Matthew 24:12). As to the
why of it we are not told. We know only that the all-wise,
omniscient God, who created this world and man, has
permitted it to be so. The *mystery* of evil in God's
universe is an area into which our finite minds cannot
enter. We know also that evil is here to stay until Christ

returns to reign on earth. As long as the Church remains here she must be strict in discipline.

It Was Steadfast in Duty

Concerning the church at Ephesus Jesus said, "I know thy works and thy labour ... And hast borne, and hast patience, and for My name's sake hast laboured, and hast not fainted" (2:2-3). The commendation of this church was not restricted to soundness in doctrine and strictness in discipline. The Lord's excellent testimony tells us that this church, at least when Christ sent this letter to her, had good balance. The church was orthodox, and the orthodoxy was alive and active.

In our day there are many churches characterized by dead orthodoxy. They hold to established Biblical doctrines, but their beliefs are nothing more than cold intellectualism. There is little actual life, a lack of concern for lost souls, and a shortage of zeal for the work of the Lord. They bear a testimony to what they believe but their faith is not translated into practical everyday living for the Lord.

A spirit of dogged perseverance and tenacity is a need of the hour in church life and among Christians in general. We can do with more stick-to-itiveness. There are too many like Demas of whom Paul wrote, "Demas hath forsaken me, having loved this present world" (2 Timothy 4:10). Or like the Galatians to whom the apostle wrote, "Ye did [at one time] run well; who did hinder you?" (Galatians 5:7) Patient endurance is a necessary ingredient if God's work is to prosper. The church at Ephesus seemed to have it all. It was one of the greatest churches in the known world.

But the astonishing thing was that this amazing church had one weakness. The penetrating eyes of our Lord detected one fault.

It Was Slothful in Devotion

Jesus said, "Nevertheless I have somewhat against thee, because thou hast left thy first love" (Revelation 2:4). Their laxity was not reflected in their duties but in their devotion. It was a laxity in devotion to the Lord. Despite all their strong points the Lord detected in that wonderful church a deadly defect. It was something hidden in the inner life that the average Christian could not have detected. Outwardly they gave every evidence of being a warm and zealous group of believers, but inwardly there was a coldness. That Holy-Spirit-directed exuberance and enthusiasm for the Lord Jesus and His work were beginning to wane. Their soundness in doctrine, strictness in discipline, and steadfastness in duty were becoming routine. They had not lost their fundamentalism; they just lapsed into formalism. They had not quit their fervent laboring; they merely left their first love. The honeymoon was over.

It is significant that in the Epistle Paul wrote to the church at Ephesus, some thirty years before John wrote the letters to the seven churches, *love* is mentioned not less than fourteen times in the course of its six chapters, while *love* is mentioned only four times in the Galatian Epistle, four times in the Philippian Epistle, and three times in the

Colossian Epistle. This suggests the greatness of their sin and the gravity of Christ's complaint.

Their sinful condition was not the result of an attack from an enemy outside the church, but from a spiritual lapse in the hearts of the believers inside. It is sad indeed that a church so promising should have failed so lamentably in its attitude toward the One who loved it and had given Himself for it. The first of the seven letters shows the church in its earliest beginnings going from good to bad. And the Lord was fully aware of the defect.

We have a similar condition in our churches today, and we seem to prefer it that way. Church members will attend a Sunday service with a fair amount of regularity, give towards the operating expenses, even get involved in activities; but they like it just dull and drab enough so as not to be too demanding. It wasn't always like that; but that first love for the Saviour and the saints is gone. Their orthodoxy is retained, but at great cost. Their love no longer has depth and devotion. The defect is not a matter of the head but of the heart. This is the history of the Church, and it is one reason why she cannot bring in the kingdom. A perfect society is not possible where there is an imperfect Church. That is one of the msyteries in the seven parables and seven letters our Lord revealed to His own.

John was writing to the second generation of Christians since the church at Ephesus was founded thirty years before. During that time this cooling of their first spiritual love for the Lord was gradually being replaced by a love for the things of the world. Both Paul and John warned in their writings of the danger of waning love. It is the one sin that can creep in slowly, unnoticed by any of us. Because the Adamic nature is never eradicated from the believer in Christ, we are always in danger of drifting away from the singleness and simplicity and sanctity of that first experience of the love of espousal. For, after all, "first love" is the submission and surrender of love to the greatest Lover, our Lord and Saviour Jesus Christ.

Money and the things it can purchase are often the downfall of a devoted and zealous child of God. In Paul's first Epistle to Timothy he said, "But they that will be rich fall into temptation and a snare, and into many foolish and hurtful lusts, which drown men in destruction and perdition. For the love of money is the root of all evil: which while some coveted after, they have erred from the faith, and pierced themselves through with many sorrows" (1 Timothy 6:9-10). In these two verses Paul presents *the peril of pursuing wealth*.

Then Paul adds a word to those persons who had already acquired wealth: "Charge them that are rich in this world, that they be not highminded, nor trust in uncertain riches, but in the living God, who giveth us richly all things to enjoy" (1 Timothy 6:17). In this verse he warns of *the peril of possessing wealth*.

Finally, Paul tells Timothy to charge them who possess this world's goods, "that they do good, that they be rich in good works, ready to distribute, willing to communicate; Laying up in store for themselves a good foundation against the time to come, that they may lay hold on eternal life" (1 Timothy 6:18-19). Here we are shown *the plan for perpetuating wealth*.

Beware of the *love* of money. Jesus said, "No servant

can serve two masters: for either he will hate the one, and love the other; or else he will hold to the one, and despise the other. Ye cannot serve God and mammon'' (Luke 16:13).

Similarly the Apostle John wrote, ''Love not the world, neither the things that are in the world. If any man love the world, the love of the Father is not in him'' (1 John 2:15). The world system (this present order of human affairs) is described as ''evil'' (Galatians 1:4). Satan is its god (2 Corinthians 4:4; Ephesians 6:12). Its subjects are the hosts of unbelieving men and women, many of whom are educated, refined, intellectual, cultured, wealthy, and even religious, but lost. It is indeed true that ''the whole world [system] lieth in wickedness [the wicked one]'' (1 John 5:19). The Apostle James said, ''Ye adulterers and adulteresses, know ye not that the friendship of the world is enmity with God? whosoever therefore will be a friend of the world is the enemy of God'' (James 4:4).

Some Steps To Avoid Disaster

To correct the spiritual departure and avert disaster, the Lord offered the following words of counsel: ''Remember therefore from whence thou art fallen, and repent, and do the first works; or else I will come unto thee quickly, and will remove thy candlestick out of his place, except thou repent'' (Revelation 2:5). The first steps back are simple, not difficult. Three simple words tell the story. They are *remember, repent,* and *return.*

Remember! Stop, think, and reflect upon your earliest Christian experience. Remind yourself of that new and wonderful relationship with the Lord Jesus Christ. Keep before you the fact that this word of counsel was not spoken to persons who never were born again, but to Christ's own. He is telling all of us who are His that memory is a step back to a full and fruitful fellowship with Himself.

Repent! They were to change their attitude and actions in regard to Christ and His work. When upon reflecting on your past you discover where you went wrong, don't become bitter and resentful. Don't grieve. Make up your mind that you were wrong and that you will do everything necessary to go back to that which is right. When the prodigal son "came to himself" he reflected on what he had left behind when he broke fellowship with his father. Then he said, "I will arise and go to my father, and will say unto him, Father, I have sinned against heaven, and before thee." He *remembered* and *repented*.

Return! True repentance will never drive a Christian to despair, but it will lead him to cast himself upon the grace and mercy of God. That in turn will bring him back to fellowship and fruitfulness. On more than one occasion this has been my own personal experience. I find it difficult to put into words the heights of joy and peace to which I was lifted upon repenting and returning to the Lord. God said to Jeremiah, "Go and proclaim these words toward the north, and say, *Return*, thou backsliding Israel, saith the LORD; and I will not cause Mine anger to fall upon you: for I am merciful, saith the LORD, and I will not keep anger for ever" (Jeremiah 3:12). Through the Prophet Hosea the Lord said, "O Israel, *return* unto the LORD thy God.... I will heal their backsliding, I will love them freely: for Mine anger is turned away from him'' (Hosea 14:1,4).

The sad and tragic fact remains that the church in Ephesus failed to heed the Lord's counsel. Its members had gotten caught in the vortex of the prevailing worldly spirit in that city. Their soundness in doctrine, strictness in discipline, and stedfastness to duty were insufficient in themselves to maintain a strong witness for Christ. Without love their message became as sounding brass. By the sixth century the church at Ephesus had lost its influence entirely. Today the city lies in ruins, uninhabited. Christ removed the lampstand. Their light had gone out.

Though the correspondence between the first parable in Matthew 13 and the first epistle in Revelation 2 is not so easily discernable as in the subsequent ones, the following is suggestive:

The cause of failure in the first parable was threefold. First, the seed which fell by the wayside was devoured by the emissaries of Satan. Secondly, the seed which fell upon stony places, though springing up, yet through lack of depth of earth, and hence absence of root, was scorched by the sun. Thirdly, the seed which fell among thorns was choked by the cares of this world and the deceitfulness of riches.

The cause of failure in the first church was threefold. First, they failed to depend upon the Lord's presence and power in their midst; secondly, a consequent departure from their first love; thirdly, the usurping of the Church's Head by human leaders.

The leading lesson in both parable and epistle is the same, namely, failure. A disaster during the sowing time cannot produce a perfect crop at harvest time. Therefore, as we proceed to examine the remaining letters to as many churches, we will not be surprised to learn that failure in Christ's Church must result in declension, until at last the apostasy spreads and the professing church is rejected by Him.

According to the prophetical view this first church represents the apostolic church of the first century, from her beginning about 30 A.D. to approximately 160 A.D.

13

THE LETTER TO SMYRNA

POVERTY WITH PLENTY

And unto the angel of the church in Smyrna write; These things saith the first and the last, which was dead, and is alive; I know thy works, and tribulation, and poverty, (but thou art rich) and I know the blasphemy of them which say they are Jews, and are not, but are the synagogue of Satan. Fear none of those things which thou shalt suffer: behold, the devil shall cast some of you into prison, that ye may be tried; and ye shall have tribulation ten days: be thou faithful unto death, and I will give thee a crown of life. He that hath an ear, let him hear what the Spirit saith unto the churches; He that overcometh shall not be hurt of the second death (Revelation 2:8-11).

In the seven letters to the seven churches we are reading our Lord's personal correspondence to the leaders in each church. Apparently Jesus saw in these particular churches a combination of the strengths and weaknesses that would be characteristic of all churches during the church age while He is absent from the earth. The principle lessons are much the same as He set forth in the seven parables in Matthew 13. It is to be regretted that so few Christians read and study these letters, because in them one finds both a prophetic and personal application.

The city of Smyrna was a beautiful city situated about

thirty-seven miles north of Ephesus. Its unusually fine seaport helped to make it a thriving business and industrial center. Having a prosperous economy, there was in Smyrna a wealthy and influential class of people, many Jews being among them. Our Lord made special reference to some of those Jews. Also in Smyrna there was an assembly of believers worshiping and serving the Lord Jesus Christ. This church was singled out by Christ to receive the second of the seven letters. The city of Smyrna, now called Izmir, stands today (1978) with a population of approximately 335,000 people. Reportedly there are close to 60,000 professing Christians.

It Was a Persecuted Church

Mentioned only here in the King James Version of Scripture, Smyrna was known for its opposition to the Christian gospel. However, it should be noted that the word appears in three other New Testament passages where it is translated *myrrh*. When the wise men came from the East to worship the child Jesus, "they presented unto Him gifts; gold, and frankincense, and myrrh [Greek, *smyrna*]" (Matthew 2:11). The gold is a type of His deity. The frankincense is a picture of His great high-priestly ministry of intercession for us. The myrrh (*smyrna*) speaks of our Lord's suffering for our sins. In the Biblical account of Christ's sufferings and crucifixion we are told that "they gave Him to drink wine mingled with myrrh [*smyrna*]: but He received it not" (Mark 15:23). Myrrh was used as one of the ingredients for the embalming of Christ's body to prepare it for His burial (John 19:39).

Thus we can see that myrrh is associated with suffering and death.

Smyrna is the church, therefore, of great persecution and suffering. In His letter to that church, Jesus said, "I know thy ... tribulation.... Fear none of those things which thou shalt suffer: behold, the devil shall cast some of you into prison, that ye may be tried; and ye shall have tribulation ten days: be thou faithful unto death, and I will give thee a crown of life" (Revelation 2:9-10). The word in the original for "tribulation" (Greek, *thlipsis*) suggests a condition of severe oppression, a persecution which was well-nigh unbearable. No church in that part of the world suffered trials and tribulations equal to those suffered by the Christians at Smyrna.

Smyrna characterizes the period of the great persecution. There were ten of them. Among the emperors who ruled over the Roman Empire, ten of them made it their business to persecute the Christians: Nero, Domitian, Trojan, Antoninus, Severus, Maximim, Decius, Valerian, Aurelian, and Diocletian. For nearly 300 years pagan rulers heaped suffering and death upon the followers of Christ. Under the direction of those godless monarchs portions of the Holy Scripture were destroyed. If we look at the church at Smyrna as representative of the Church in persecution in the second and third centuries, then the ten specific persecutions under the ten Roman emperors could be the prophetic fulfillment of Christ's words, "ye shall have tribulation ten days" (2:10). The history of the Christian Church contains the record of thousands who chose to die rather than denounce their faith in the Lord Jesus Christ.

One of the most publicized martyrdoms was that of Polycarp, bishop of Smyrna. In A.D. 155, at the time of the public games, when the city was overcrowded with visitors and excitement was running high, Polycarp was burned at the stake. He was offered his freedom if he would merely say the three words, "Caesar is Lord." But Polycarp was adamant in his loyalty to Jesus Christ. His last words were, "Eighty and six years have I served Him and He has done me no wrong. How can I blaspheme my King who saved me?" So the crowds gathered with faggots, and the venerable saint died in the flames.

Among the persecutors at that time were Jews living in Smyrna. When Jesus informed the church that He was acquainted with the persecution they were suffering, He added, "And I know the blasphemy of them which say they are Jews, and are not, but are the synagogue of Satan" (2:9). Certain Jews frequently succeeded in stirring up the authorities to take action against the Christians. We know this to be so according to Luke's record in the book of Acts. At Antioch "the Jews stirred up the devout and honourable women, and the chief men of the city, and raised persecution against Paul and Barnabas, and expelled them out of their coasts" (Acts 13:50). It happened again at Iconium (Acts 14:1-5), at Lystra (Acts 14:19), and at Thessalonica (Acts 17:5).

Jesus called that particular group of Jews "the synagogue of Satan," a term He used again in His letter to the church at Philadelphia (Revelation 3:9). In Greek the word *synagogue* is *sunagōgē*, which literally means a gathering together, an assembly (Numbers 16:3; 20:4; 31:16). In substance Jesus is saying of those Jews in

Smyrna, "They call themselves the assembly of God, when in reality they are the assembly of the devil." Once He said to the religious Pharisees, "ye are of your father the devil" (John 8:44).

Those blasphemers in Smyrna no doubt belonged to the nation of Israel, so that in a national sense they were the children of Abraham. Because they were the children of Abraham according to the flesh, they claimed to be the true children of God, but in reality they were imposters. The Apostle Paul, himself a Jew, wrote, "For he is not a Jew, which is one outwardly; neither is that circumcision, which is outward in the flesh: But he is a Jew, which is one inwardly; and circumcision is that of the heart, in the spirit, and not in the letter; whose praise is not of men, but of God" (Romans 2:28-29). The hatred of the Jews in Smyrna toward the Christians there was principally their hatred toward Christ. They did not believe in Christ. They rejected Him and despised the Christian message of justification through faith in Christ's substitutionary death on the cross. Satan was their leader, who inspired them in all of their slander. As the opponent of the one true God and of Christ, Satan had gained leadership in the synagogue of the Jews at Smyrna. They contributed in a larger measure to the persecution of the believers in that city.

It Was a Poor Church

Jesus said, "I know thy ... poverty, (but thou art rich)" (Revelation 2:9). Spiritually the church of Smyrna was rich, but materially and socially they were poor. They were denied business opportunities and social contacts, all of which added to the existing hardship they were suffering. A Christian in business might have his shop boycotted, or be dismissed by his employer. What the Christians in Smyrna experienced was but a foretaste of the persecution to be encountered during the tribulation under the rule of Antichrist.

In the church of Smyrna Satan had introduced his tares. A dark shadow had fallen over God's wheat field. But then our Lord had warned His disciples that the tares would appear in the same field with the wheat throughout this entire age. They should not have been surprised at the persecution and poverty they were suffering. Satan and his emissaries are never friends to God's people. They have infiltrated churches all throughout church history and will continue to do so until the end of the age. During the first three centuries material poverty was a part of the Church's persecution and tribulation. But this should not have taken the Christians by surprise, because Jesus had warned His disciples, "In the world ye shall have tribulation" (John 16:33). "If the world hate you, ye know that it hated Me before it hated you. If ye were of the world, the world would love his own: but because ye are not of the world, but I have chosen you out of the world, therefore the world hateth you. Remember the word that I said unto you, The servant is not greater than his lord. If they have persecuted Me, they will also persecute you; if they have kept My saying, they will keep yours also" (John 15:18-20). Both persecution and poverty were a part of our Lord's life.

When Jesus said, "I know thy ... tribulation, and

poverty'' (Revelation 2:9), He did not use the word *ginōskō*, which frequently means to know, in the sense of realizing through progress in knowledge. He used the word *oida*, which suggests fullness of knowledge, to know perfectly, not merely from observation, but from experience. Though suffering saints are unknown to the world and hated by the world, they are known to the Lord and loved by Him. Christ knows the persecution and poverty of His own; He knows how the world looks upon them. Many a tired, tried, and troubled saint has been strengthened and encouraged by those two monosyllables, *I know*. Those two words uttered by our Saviour touch our troubles with the smile of God, and make this world's suffering ''not worthy to be compared with the glory which shall be revealed in us'' (Romans 8:18).

The churches of the first three centuries were marked by persecution and poverty. Today churches and Christian organizations are known for their popularity and wealth. Recently (June 28, 1977) I read an Associated Press release that the world's best-known and most-popular evangelist amassed a shielded fund of $23 million in land, blue-chip stocks, bonds, and cash. In our affluent society there are some church-related and religious groups that are blighted with an abundance of wealth. They will frequently attribute their wealth to ''the blessing of the Lord.'' By such standards the church at Smyrna was not blessed by God. We all need to be reminded that the devil and his crowd are not poor.

Perhaps we might take another look at the Church's Head as He lived on our earth. When a certain scribe volunteered to follow our Lord, Jesus said to him, ''The foxes have holes, and the birds of the air have nests; but the Son of man hath not where to lay His head'' (Matthew 8:20). Paul said, ''For your sakes He became poor'' (2 Corinthians 8:9).

Now I am not suggesting that God puts a premium on poverty. Nor am I intimating that poverty is a sign of spirituality. I have met and known some of God's choice children who prospered greatly in material wealth. They came by their wealth honestly and disposed of it scripturally. Many missionaries who went to foreign lands practically penniless were supported by Christians here at home, men and women who worked hard and earned enough money to support themselves as well as others. Let us thank God for them. Their reward awaits them. I am merely trying to point out that in our Lord's letter to Smyrna there is not one word of criticism, only beautiful words of comfort and commendation. Yet that church was persecuted and poor.

It Was a Privileged Church

Don't pass lightly over those four words in parentheses, ''(*but thou art rich*)'' (Revelation 2:9). Here is one of the great paradoxes in the Bible. Jesus said, ''I know thy ... poverty, (but thou art rich).'' Here is a seeming contradiction that is contrary to worldly opinion. It is opposed to common sense, and yet it is true. But someone might ask, ''If the church at Smyrna was poor, wherein did its wealth lie?'' When Jesus said they were rich, He meant they were rich in *faith* (James 2:5). I know this because that church pleased the Lord, and ''without faith it is impossible to please Him'' (Hebrews 11:6). Now an individual or a church can be rich or poor in material things and still please God, but not many do. It is interesting to note that the church at Smyrna did not have any of the weaknesses nor signs of deterioration found in other churches. Why? They were rich in faith, and ''rich in good works'' (1 Timothy 6:18). They possessed a spiritual enrichment.

What a contrast between the church of Smyrna and the church of Laodicea! In Smyrna there was the poor church the Lord called rich. In Laodicea there was the rich church He called poor. Christ's letter to the rich church in Laodicea must have pierced like an arrow when He said, ''Because thou sayest, I am rich, and increased with goods, and have need of nothing; and knowest not that thou art wretched, and miserable, and poor, and blind, and naked'' (Revelation 3:17). This was the church that was nauseating to the Lord. She was so disgusting the Lord was ready to reject her. The tragedy in that rich church lay in the fact that she was smug, complacent, self-satisfied, and would not admit to her own wretchedness. She was blinded by her material wealth. The root of her life was not faith. She could not say, ''We walk by faith, not by sight'' (2 Corinthians 5:7). Nor could she say, ''We look not at the things which are seen, but at the things which are not seen: for the things which are seen are temporal; but the things which are not seen are eternal'' (2 Corinthians 4:18).

Yes, the church at Smyrna was rich in faith, and by faith she was linked to her Head, who walked in the midst of the churches. Because she was strong in faith she grew in grace and increased in spiritual wealth. Her persecution and poverty only tended to exercise and strengthen her faith. When a church is genuinely faithful in its doctrine and deportment it will not be popular with the world.

When a church is wealthy and honored by the world, it will attract tares as well as wheat. It becomes a matter of pride to become a member of such a church. After a while carnal Christians and even the unsaved join that church and become a veritable danger to it. It is not too long until their carnal desires and worldly behavior are imposed upon that church. Wherever you find a church that is suffering persecution and reproach for Christ's sake, it will be cleansed of these religious Pharisees.

Should the church deliberately stir up the world to make it hate and persecute us? The answer to such a question is an emphatic *no!* If the church is sincerely dedicated to sound belief and behavior in the midst of a wicked world system, the world will naturally hate her. No Christian can be totally dedicated to Jesus Christ and be popular with the world. After our Lord saved Saul of Tarsus, He said, ''I will show him how great things he must suffer for My name's sake'' (Acts 9:16). And suffer Paul did, possibly as much as any Christian ever suffered for Christ. When Paul listed some of the tribulations he suffered, he added, ''as poor, yet making many rich; as having nothing, and yet possessing all things'' (2 Corinthians 6:10). The great apostle, like the Christians at Smyrna, was a privileged saint, poor yet rich.

But the greatest blessing that enriched the lives of the poor Christians at Smyrna was the presence of Christ in their midst. His opening words in His letter speak of

Himself as "the first and the last, which was dead, and is alive" (Revelation 2:8). This description of our Lord is a repetition of the one He gave to John earlier (1:11,18). This church is in the midst of persecution and poverty, which will result in death for some of its members. So He reminds them that He experienced it all, having overcome death. He only could say, "I am He that liveth, and was dead; and, behold, I am alive for evermore, Amen; and have the keys of hell and of death" (1:18). He has defeated the enemy and is now Master over every situation. To the Christian who is suffering, this is a tremendous asset. Come what may, from the beginning of our Christian experience to the last day of life on earth, the risen Lord who overcame persecution and death is with His own.

During this church dispensation no Christian should expect that life will be free from problems or persecution. We Christians of this twentieth century have no right to suppose that life for us will be easier than it was for our brothers and sisters in Christ in the first three centuries. Jesus did not promise the church at Smyrna deliverance from their problems, but He did assure them that He, the mighty Victor, would be with them. As the One who suffered and died and conquered death, He can give the faithful members of His Church comfort and courage and hope. This tells us that we are the privileged rich in this world.

The self-introduction of our Lord to each of the seven churches is harmonious with the state of each church at the time the seven letters were written. However, even though those stages of history are, for the most part, in the past, those same conditions appear from time to time and in various places even to our own day. In communist countries today Christians are subjected to severe persecution. We in America can expect increasing pressure upon Christ's Church as we move steadily to a socialistic form of government. For those Christians living when the pressures and persecutions do come, we know that it will be a temporary experience, a brief episode, a passing phase. When Christ suffered, became dead, and came to life again, it was for Him a passing phase, a brief episode that lasted for a short period of time. He who experienced the worst the enemy could do conquered the worst the enemy could do. He is the Head of His Church today and always will be.

If you are one of Christ's and confess Him as your Saviour and Lord, there is a definite and personal relationship between Him and you. Never deny that relationship nor be ashamed of His name. In times of prosperity and popularity it will not be difficult openly to confess that you love and serve Him. It will call for little faithfulness on your part to confess Him then. But you must be prepared to face more difficult days ahead when, because of His name, you will be the object of scorn and reproach of this world, when your public confession of Christ could result in severe persecution. To you and to me He says, ''Be thou faithful unto death, and I will give thee a crown of life'' (2:10).

No doubt some of you have heard or read Corrie Ten Boom's account of her experiences in concentration camps. A group of Christians had gathered in a church building to worship the Lord Jesus Christ. They were in an iron curtain country. Suddenly the church door was thrust open and two Russian soldiers with submachine guns walked in. They called the Christians to attention and said they would give five minutes for anyone who wanted to renounce Christ to leave, and that those who remained would be shot immediately. A few walked out of the church, but the majority remained. Then the soldiers locked the door of the church, turned to the Christians and said, "Brothers and sisters in Christ, we are believers, but we did not want to worship where anyone was not completely committed to Jesus Christ and willing to die for Him."

It is possible that our loyalty to Christ will bring us persecution and poverty, but we are rich, the privileged rich who will surely receive the crown of life. What difference does it make how the world treats us, so long as we have with us Him who said, "I will never leave thee, nor forsake thee" (Hebrews 13:5)?

As we look back into church history, the Smyrna church covers that period from about 160 A.D. to approximately 312 A.D. It was the time when Christianity was under persecution in the Roman Empire. In this letter, as in all seven letters and in the seven parables in Matthew 13, we see history in prophecy.

14

THE LETTER TO PERGAMOS

CONFESSING YET COMPROMISING

And to the angel of the church in Pergamos write: These things saith He which hath the sharp sword with two edges. I know thy works, and where thou dwellest, even where Satan's seat is; and thou holdest fast My name, and hast not denied My faith, even in those days wherein Antipas was My faithful martyr, who was slain among you, where Satan dwelleth. But I have a few things against thee, because thou hast there them that hold the doctrine of Balaam, who taught Balac to cast a stumbling block before the children of Israel, to eat things sacrificed unto idols, and to commit fornication. So hast thou also them that hold the doctrine of the Nicolaitans, which thing I hate. Repent; or else I will come unto thee quickly, and will fight against them with the sword of My mouth. He that hath an ear, let him hear what the Spirit saith unto the churches: To him that overcometh will I give to eat of the hidden manna, and will give him a white stone, and in the stone a new name written, which no man knoweth saving he that receiveth it (Revelation 2:12-17).

This third letter is addressed to the church in Pergamos, or as the Greeks called it, Pergamum. It was a rather large city situated farther north some forty miles distant from Smyrna. It was the foremost and therefore the most famous of the three cities we have yet considered. Industry, science, and art found their home there, and all of this attracted many famous and learned Greeks. Pergamos possessed a library which was second only to the library of fame at Alexandria.

Secular history informs us that Pergamos was a wealthy city with many elaborate and costly temples and cathedrals devoted to idol worship. Sacred groves, statues, and altars were common throughout the city. There were four gorgeous, impressive temples to the four famous Greek gods: Zeus, Dionysius, Athena, and Aesculapius. This latter god was the most famous, known all over the ancient world as the god of healing, the Pergamene god. His imposing temple attracted the sick and suffering from many parts of the known civilized world.

Pergamos became known as a pantheon of pagan worship, the seat of sacred sensuality. Our Lord referred to it as the place "where Satan's seat is" (Revelation 2:13). That word translated "seat" is the Greek word *thronos*, so that Christ said to the church, "I know ... where thou dwellest ... where Satan's [throne] is." The city is pictured to us as being a stronghold of the devil, the base of his evil operations where he held undisputed sway. Even the emblem of the god Aesculapius was a serpent. A throne in Scripture occurs frequently as the symbol of authority and dominion. Here is a city pictured to us as being dominated by the satanic power of opposition, a stronghold of the prince of darkness.

In this atmosphere, totally opposed to Christ and the Christian testimony, stood a little assembly of believers known as "the church in Pergamos." It is the church Christ established in the midst of the fiercest opposition to Himself and His followers. It is true of this entire dispensation that the whole world system lies in the wicked one, and that the kingdoms of this world are under his dominion (1 John 5:19). Our Lord Himself called Satan "the prince of this world" (John 12:31; 14:30; 16:11). To this Paul added a descriptive term of Satan as "the god of this world" (2 Corinthians 4:4). While in other places throughout the world Satan and his demons manifested his presence and power, in a special sense his headquarters were in Pergamos. He dwelled where Christ had planted a Christian witness. Pergamos was in that day Satan's capital, and particularly hostile to the Christian faith.

The opening words of the risen Christ to His little flock in Pergamos were, "These things saith He which hath the sharp sword with two edges" (Revelation 2:12). This is the description of Christ that John saw earlier in 1:16. We have already pointed out that the character in which our Lord presented Himself to these churches is in strict accord with their various conditions and needs. To the church at Ephesus He revealed Himself as the One walking in the midst of the seven lampstands and holding in His hand the seven stars. This indicated His presence with, and absolute authority over, all the members of His Church. To the church at Smyrna He made Himself known as "the first and the last, which was dead, and is alive." This title was primarily intended to act as a word of comfort and consolation to those who were to suffer death for their faith in Christ. But here He is writing to a church that is not suffering persecution and martyrdom, but which faces temptation of a different nature.

"The sharp sword with two edges" is clearly the *Word*

of God. Reference is made to this holy blade several times in the Bible. This is possibly the meaning of Simeon's words to Mary, "Yea, a sword shall pierce through thy own soul also" (Luke 2:35). Paul said, "Take the ... sword of the Spirit, which is the Word of God" (Ephesians 6:17). "For the Word of God is quick, and powerful, and sharper than any twoedged sword, piercing even to the dividing asunder of soul and spirit, and of the joints and marrow, and is a discerner of the thoughts and intents of the heart" (Hebrews 4:12). Christ called it "the sword of My mouth" (Revelation 2:16). It is His own Word with which He will smite the nations (Revelation 19:15,21). The sword, then, is Christ's own Word of truth, a description of Him that fits perfectly the need in the church at Pergamos.

The character and condition of the visible church in Pergamos, as revealed by Christ, outlines the third period of the Church's history and corresponds exactly with the third parable in Matthew 13. It shows a further advance in Satan's methods of attack upon Christ and His Church. In this third historic period of the Church's history, Satan entirely changed his tactics. During the Smyrna period of the Christian profession he used weapons of force in an attempt to bring about the Church's destruction. Christians were cast into prison, mercilessly tortured, and killed. But the gates of hell could not prevail against the Church. Satan now appears with a different approach. But first, we must proceed a step at a time in examining our Lord's comments describing conditions in the church at Pergamos.

Christ Commends Their Confession

"I know thy works, and where thou dwellest, even where Satan's seat is: and thou holdest fast My name, and hast not denied My faith, even in those days wherein Antipas was My faithful martyr, who was slain among you, where Satan dwelleth" (2:13). In our day there are those who might insist that it is advisable for the church to move out of that wicked city where the devil has his headquarters. I'm sure that many of us, at one time or another, felt it would be much easier to serve the Lord in some other location and in other circumstances where bearing a witness would be easier. But the Scriptures do not tell us that the Church should emigrate from the world and live in isolation. Her members might be more safe in some other locations, but that is not God's plan for her. He wants the name of His Son honored and confessed in the midst of devilish and wicked surroundings.

Someone might ask, what is so important about holding fast the name of the Lord Jesus Christ? Holding fast that name includes a personal loyalty to and faith in the Person and work of Christ. The Christian must confess Christ, for not to confess Him is to deny Him. He Himself said, "Whosoever therefore shall confess Me before men, him will I confess also before My Father which is in heaven. But whosoever shall deny Me before men, him will I also deny before My Father which is in heaven" (Matthew 10:32-33). The name of the Lord Jesus Christ stands for Himself, His deity, His sinlessness, His atoning work for sinners through His death on the cross, His bodily resurrection from death and the grave, His ascension to Heaven, and the fact of His return to earth. In these days Christ's name is blasphemed and caricatured in almost every area of life: political, educational, social, religious. Yes, even in the religious life of our great country there are those persons who are prostituting that holy name for material gain. Our Lord warned, "Many will say to Me in that day, Lord, Lord, have we not prophesied in Thy name? and in Thy name have cast out devils? and in Thy name done many wonderful works? And then will I profess unto them, I never knew you: depart from Me, ye that work iniquity" (Matthew 7:22-23). Let us never utter His name lightly or loosely, but hold it at all times in the highest respect and reverence.

Christ commended the church in Pergamos further when He said, "Thou hast not denied My faith" (Revelation 2:13). He praises the believers for their doctrinal faithfulness as they dwelt in the shadow of Satan's throne. They could have denied the faith by refusing to confess it, by attempting to go underground as so-called secret believers. But they refused to hide their light under a bushel. The Christians at Pergamos proved that it was possible to bear a witness for Christ under the most adverse surroundings and satanic opposition. In spite of that evil environment, the Pergamos believers held fast to Christ's name and did not deny His faith. They were loyal, not only to the Person of Christ, but to His total teaching. After all, He is "the author and finisher of ... faith" (Hebrews 12:2). His faith has become the life principle of all redeemed persons.

As an example of the faithfulness of the saints in Pergamos, the Lord mentions one of the early martyrs, named Antipas. Of this faithful witness for Christ we know nothing. His name does not appear in secular history, but we shall meet him in Heaven and witness his receiving the crown of life. The risen Lord called Antipas "My faithful martyr." The Greek word *martus* is translated *martyr* in the English Bible, but in fact it is the normal Greek word for *witness*. In the early Church a witness and a martyr were one and the same thing. When a person became a Christian he knew that his witness of Jesus Christ exposed him to actual martyrdom. He was prepared to prove his love for Christ by dying for Him if called upon to do so. Oftentimes it cost much to be a Christian in those early days of the Church. Then one would accept death rather than deny the Lord who redeemed him. The name and faith of the Lord Jesus Christ were more precious than life itself.

Christ Condemns Their Compromise

An error crept into the church at Pergamos that overbalanced their confession. The Lord said, "But I have a few things against thee, because thou hast there them that hold the doctrine of Balaam, who taught Balac to cast a stumblingblock before the children of Israel, to eat things sacrificed unto idols, and to commit fornication. So hast thou also them that hold the doctrine of the Nicolaitans, which thing I hate" (Revelation 2:14-15).

This third epistle, addressed to the church at Pergamos, had in it an error which aptly delineated the character and condition of the visible church in the third historic phase of its existence. As was stated earlier, it corresponds exactly with the third parable in Matthew 13 and it also shows a further advance in Satan's methods of attack upon the woman's Seed. During this period of the Church's history Satan entirely changed his tactics. During the Smyrna period of the Christian profession the devil used weapons of force against Christ's followers, a move that was unsuccessful. The fiercer the fires of affliction, the firmer was the faith of those Christians. Satan could not crush their indomitable spirit. We are now to see plainly Satan's subtlety, his wiles and wisdom.

One of the errors that crept into the Pergamos assembly was "the doctrine of Balaam." The church that dwells under the shadow of Satan's throne will be exposed to Satan's fiery darts. Bearing down on the Christians at Smyrna the enemy came "as a roaring lion" (1 Peter 5:8) to curse and to crush. But here he smiles upon Pergamos as an angel of light (2 Corinthians 11:14). His weapon was "the doctrine of Balaam," the counsel of a shrewd and clever prophet who caused God's people to lose something good they have never since regained.

What was the doctrine of Balaam? It was the teaching of a compromise in life that brought corruption. The account of Balaam is recorded in Numbers 22:1—25:9. Balaam had the gift of prophecy but, like many prophets of whom our Lord spoke in Matthew 7:22-23, he came to a sorry end. He spoke God's Word with his mouth while in his heart there was a satanic covetousness that reached out for the rewards and riches of this world.

Balak, king of Moab, offered Balaam a good wage if he would pronounce a curse upon Israel. At first Balaam rejected Balak's offer (Numbers 22:5-13), but when

Balak's messenger came a second time with a larger offer and greater fringe benefits, Balaam accepted (Numbers 22:14-21). Three times he tried to pronounce a curse upon Israel, but each time the Lord restrained him. Not to be denied the handsome fee offered by Balak, Balaam conceived the evil plan that was to bring to pass Israel's downfall. Knowing that he could not *curse* God's people, he proposed to *corrupt* them. His method was one of subtle infiltration. He suggested that the pretty Moabite girls should date the young men of Israel. The Moabite women succeeded and they did their work well. Through that unholy alliance, that unequal yoke, Israel fell. Balaam had followed Satan's old line. When *murder* fails (Genesis 4), try *mixture* (Genesis 6). This is the unequal yoke (2 Corinthians 6:14).

Just as Balaam showed Balak how Israel could be hindered from receiving God's promised blessing, even so the Church, in that third period of her history, was hindered by the infiltration of the doctrine of Balaam. Early in the fourth century the evil principle of Balaamism crept into the assembly at Pergamos. After the death of Diocletian, Constantine became the ruling monarch of the Roman Empire. He declared himself a Christian and made Christianity the religion of the state. He was carried on a golden throne to the church council as the recognized head of the church. But in spite of his profession, and the pomp and ceremony that accompanied it, there was no evidence that he had ever been born again. During that period in the Church's history the world infiltrated the church. In the Pergamos stage of history the church became wedded to the world. Great numbers of persons were baptized and brought into the church who never knew the experience of regeneration. They were merely professing Christians. Declaring one's self a Christian was the popular thing to do. It was the "in" thing.

Instead of being hated and despised, Christians were now accepted, made to feel welcome and wanted in the political, business, and social life of the city. In a few generations the church and the world were one. It soon became difficult to distinguish the Christians from those who were not Christians. The compromise of Christians became increasingly obvious as the church began to join the world in crime and bloody wars. The mixing of the church and the world was Satan's new strategy.

This is exactly what our Lord predicted in the parable of the mustard seed. That parable teaches an unnatural and unhealthy development. Believers and unbelievers are joined in one big religious monstrosity. It is religious but not truly and totally Christian. The mustard seed that became a tree is a false greatness. It is great in numbers, influence, and wealth but not in spiritual strength. The "birds of the air" in that great tree represented Satan and his agents. Many are being drawn to it through the efforts of the ecumenical church. It continues to grow, spreading its branches and inviting all to unite with it. The worldly and the wealthly, the religious and the poor are urged to it. And it all began when the Church compromised with the world. In both the parable of the mustard seed and the letter to Pergamos our Lord predicted the character and course of this present age. What persecution could not accomplish in Smyrna, Satan did accomplish through the teaching of Balaam. Thus Christ labeled the church at

Pergamos as the compromising church.

Our Lord's indictment of the church at Pergamos makes clear the fact that Christians must remain pure and separate from the world and its defilements. The religious and moral standards of the world system are far removed from those of genuine Christianity. The doctrine of the Nicolaitans, which is a moral departure, and one which Christ said He hated (Revelation 2:6), ought not to be practiced by any child of God. That which the Ephesian church was commended for hating became accepted by some in the church at Pergamos (2:6). This is one of the evil results when worldly, unregenerated persons are received into the church as Christians. The conscience of the church becomes blurred, and Biblical simplicity is replaced by a complex and perplexing ecclesiastical organization.

In spite of Christ's warning (2:16), the apostasy which invaded the church at Pergamos has continued. We have men in our pulpits who actually promote what they call "the new morality," which is in reality the old pagan immorality with a new label on it. There should be no misunderstanding of the fact that the world is the enemy of Christ and His Church. "Ye adulterers and adulteresses, know ye not that the friendship of the world is enmity with God? whosoever therefore will be a friend of the world is the enemy of God" (James 4:4). Right here the church at Pergamos failed. From A.D. 313 till the rise of the papacy, about A.D. 600, the church became wealthy but worldly, influential but insipid, popular but powerless. It was a dark day in church history when the sacred corridors of the Church were trampled by the defiling feet of the world.

The prophecy in this letter commenced its fulfillment early in the fourth century and continues to our day. The church age is witnessing Christendom being taken over by the ecumenical church, that religious monstrosity which is a poor likeness of Christ's true Church. The story of the church's unholy alliance with the world and her subsequent failure is a matter of history. Unil our Lord returns, Satan's throne and dwelling place will continue in this world. He will continue to infiltrate the schools, colleges, universities, seminaries, and churches. Christ will be humanized and man will be deified. Surely in our day the prince of darkness has his dwelling place in the midst of the Christian society. And tragedy of tragedies, the relation of the church to the world in the latter part of this twentieth century is not so much different from that of the church at Pergamos in the fourth century.

No local assembly can follow the Lord and the world at the same time. When I was in Dallas, Texas, I witnessed a young woman riding two horses at the same time. She stood erect with one foot on the back of each horse as they galloped side by side around a circular ring. But I am certain that no rider can ride two horses at the same time when they are going in opposite directions. The Lord Jesus Christ and the world are going in opposite directions. Our Lord said, ''No servant can serve two masters: for either he will hate the one, and love the other; or else he will hold to the one, and despise the other. Ye cannot serve God and mammon'' (Luke 16:13). And we better believe it!

Christ Calls Them To Change

There were two distinct classes in the church at Pergamos, the true saints who were faithful and those who held the evil doctrine of Balaam. To the latter Christ said, "Repent, or else I will come unto thee quickly, and will fight against them with the sword of My mouth. He that hath an ear, let him hear what the Spirit saith unto the churches" (2:16-17). Those in the church who were guilty of compromise, the Lord held responsible.

There is then the place of repentance in the life of the Christian. When we discover that we have done wrong, the one course of action is to admit it. We must not become bitter and blame others for our sins. If we make excuses we complicate the problem and dig ourselves deeper into the mire. Saul said, "I have sinned ... I have played the fool, and have erred exceedingly" (1 Samuel 26:21). The call to repentance is a call to deal with our sin and turn from it. Repentance is a change both in attitude and action, having a real place in the life of the Christian. It is a definite condition of blessing. True repentance will never drive a Christian to despair, but it will, as in the case of the prodigal, lead him back to the Father and confess, "I have sinned" (Luke 15:18). The compromising Christian need not stay the way he is.

The appeal of Christ is to the individual. "*He* that hath an ear, let *him* hear what the Spirit saith unto the churches" (Revelation 2:17). This is a very personal matter. When any person decides to follow Christ he or she must be prepared to be different. The child of God is a set-apart person, totally different from other persons. Each of us must exercise great care lest we lapse to the level of the world. As was stated earlier in this series of studies, the Church's business is not to try to change the world, but to make known the gospel so that people will be saved and thereby delivered from the world system. But the Church becomes the object of ridicule and the finger of scorn is pointed at her when she allows herself to engage in the socializing and secularizing ways of the world.

We Christians will never suppress error by compromising with it. This was proved during the Pergamos period when the church merged with the state. What appeared to be a blessing to the church was actually a curse. In order to gain prominence and power the church compromised her position more and more. Those dark days for the church during the fourth and fifth centuries she brought upon herself when she was married to the world. It was a mixed marriage, an unequal yoke in the most objectionable sense of the word.

To this compromising church the Lord Jesus speaks, calling the guilty ones to change. Notice His discriminating words, "I will come unto *thee* ... and will fight against *them*" (2:16). He will gather the wheat to Himself but He will make war on the tares. If there is no repentance, there must be judgment.

What are we as individuals doing to keep the Church separate from the world? There are many fine, dedicated Christian men and women who work under difficult worldly conditions. It is their only means of livelihood. They are *in* the world but not *of* the world. They keep themselves "unspotted from the world" (James 1:27). But their lot in life is made more difficult by the number of people in the church who compromise with the world, persuaded that they ought to go along with the crowd. They place their social and financial status above their witness for Christ.

To the overcomer Christ promises He will ''give to eat of the hidden manna'' (Revelation 2:17). During the forty-year wandering in the wilderness God provided His people with a special food for their daily sustenance. It was called ''manna.'' Moses said, ''This is the bread which the LORD hath given you to eat'' (Exodus 16:4-15). In the process of time there was no longer a need for the manna, but God intended that the memory of it should never pass away. A pot of manna was placed (hidden) in the ark of the covenant so that future generations would be reminded of God's miraculous and merciful provision for His people (Exodus 16:32-35 cf., Hebrews 9:4). When our Lord rehearsed that historical incident, He made clear the fact that the manna was a type of Himself. He said, ''I am that bread of life.... I am the living bread which came down from heaven'' (John 6:48,51).

Christ the eternal Word incarnate is the true Bread upon whom we feed daily for sustenance. Some of the Christians at Pergamos, like many professing believers today, were feeding on the husks of this world. The manna suggests the sufficiency of Christ. The Christian who partakes daily of Christ lives above the world. When we are willing to cut ourselves off from compromising with the world, we enjoy the blessings and benefits of fellowship with Christ. This in turn strengthens the Church's witness in Satan's stronghold. We must cling to Christ. He is our all and we are complete in Him.

The correspondence between this third epistle and third parable in Matthew 13 is apparent. One is the counterpart of the other. In the fourth century the church was blinded by the attractions of the world and soon became merged into the world. Her heavenly character was lost and the great ecclesiastical mustard tree emerged. That third parable and Christ's letter to this third church are identical in meaning. They mesh into a divine pattern. As I see the tree spreading, I stand in awe before the unfolding of prophecy as it was spoken by our Lord Jesus Christ.

15

THYATIRA

THE COMMENDABLE AND THE COUNTERFEIT

And unto the angel of the church in Thyatira write; These things saith the Son of God, who hath His eyes like unto a flame of fire, and His feet are like fine brass; I know thy works, and charity, and service, and faith, and thy patience, and thy works; and the last to be more than the first. Notwithstanding I have a few things against thee, because thou sufferest that woman Jezebel, which calleth herself a prophetess, to teach and to seduce My servants to commit fornication, and to eat things sacrificed to idols. And I gave her space to repent of her fornication; and she repented not. Behold, I will cast her into a bed, and them that commit adultery with her into great tribulation, except they repent of their deeds. And I will kill her children with death; and all the churches shall know that I am He which searcheth the reins and hearts: and I will give unto every one of you according to your works. But unto you I say, and unto the rest in Thyatira, as many as have not this doctrine, and which have not known the depths of Satan, as they speak; I will put upon you none other burden. But that which ye have already hold fast till I come. And he that overcometh, and keepeth My works unto the end, to him will I give power over the nations: And he shall rule them with a rod of iron; as the vessels of a potter shall they be broken to shivers: even as I received of My Father. And I will give him the morning star. He that hath an ear, let him hear what the Spirit saith unto the churches (Revelation 2:18-29).

We have seen in our study that there is a parallel between the Biblical accounts of the seven parables in Matthew 13 and the seven churches in Revelation 2—3. Both passages contain spoken messages by our Lord and both set forth His prophetic preview of the character and course of this present age leading to His coming again, at which time He will set up His kingdom here on earth.

It has been observed further that there are valid comparisons between the Biblical account of the seven churches and the periods in church history which they represent. The featured characteristics of the seven congregations in Asia do appear to show themselves in church history. Moreover, they are manifest successively in the identical order to that which is stated in Revelation 2—3.

All of this leads me to the conclusion that these seven stages in church history consume the entire time between the two advents of Christ to earth. During the Ephesus period (30—160 A.D.), the first sign of defection in the Church was detected by the Lord. Many Christians in Ephesus had left their first love. In the Smyrna period (160—312 A.D.) satanic opposition brought persecution and poverty to many Christians. In the Pergamos period (313—600 A.D.), the church was infiltrated by the world and unregenerated persons were baptized and called Christians. In all of this we can see the three foes of Christ and His Church, namely, the flesh, the devil, and the world—in that order. This monstrous trinity of evil has been at work opposing the gospel and will continue to do so until our Lord returns.

This fourth letter, addressed to the church in Thyatira,

is no less pregnant with prophetical significance. It covers the period 600—1517 A.D. In Thyatira a major step to apostasy is taken. The leading characteristics can be traced unmistakably to both ecclesiastical· and secular history. Moreover, the correspondence between this fourth epistle and the fourth parable in Matthew 13 is apparent.

There are some unique features in this letter which are a striking change from the three which preceded it. To Ephesus and Pergamos the Lord said, "Repent" (2:5,16). Here He says that the opportunity to repent was given but there was an unwillingness to repent (2:21). To Thyatira Christ makes His first mention of His coming again (2:25). Associated with the future He announces severe judgments (2:22-23).

Something terrible happened during those nine hundred years of church history to invoke a judgment so severe. The evil that arose in Pergamos, and that came to full strength in the seventh century, continues with us today and will continue till Christ returns to judge it.

The Christ of Thyatira

Here the Lord assumes a title which He did not use in the first three epistles. "These things saith the Son of God, who hath His eyes like unto a flame of fire, and His feet are like fine brass" (2:18). This is the only church to which our Lord addressed Himself as the Son of God. The reason for the present use of this title is not difficult to see. The woeful condition of the church demanded such a revelation. The title "Son of God" signifies unrivaled supremacy, and it was this very word that the faithful remnant in Thyatira needed. It was in this church that Christ's place had been usurped and His deity virtually denied. The condition called for a reiteration of His deity.

John saw "His eyes like unto a flame of fire" (2:18). More than once—as when He beheld the city (Luke 19:41); as when He stood by the graveside of Lazarus (John 11:35); as when He looked upon Peter (Luke 22:61)—His eyes were moist with tears of concern and compassion. But here His eyes are set upon judgment as He shows His utter intolerance and abhorrence of the evil which has crept into this church. It is the eye-flame of omniscient perception penetrating and ·piercing beneath all disguises and hypocrisies. Christ only can search the hearts of men and bring to the surface the hidden things of darkness. "Neither is there any creature that is not manifest in His sight: but all things are naked and opened unto the eyes of Him with whom we have to do" (Hebrews 4:13). He knows all things and He can ferret out every evil.

"And His feet are like fine brass" (Revelation 2:18). Once those feet had been footsore, as when He rested by the well of Samaria. Once those feet had been bathed in tears and dried with the hair of a loving disciple. Once those feet had been pierced with nails and fastened to a cross. But here those glowing feet tell of endurance and strength as they symbolize irresistible divine judgment. These are the feet which will one day crush the serpent. These are the feet which will make a footstool of all His enemies. These are the feet which will one day tread the fierceness and wrath of Almighty God. His feet are beautiful to those who love Him but terrible to those who will be trodden by them. This letter is intended to be one of wrath because brass is a symbol of the righteous anger and judgment of God.

The Commendation of Thyatira

What a commendation this is! Our Lord says, "I know thy works, and charity, and service, and faith, and thy patience, and thy works; and the last to be more than the first" (2:19). It is interesting that this church was commended first for its love, especially when love is omitted from the commendations to the three preceding churches. Our Lord is unsparing in His censure but He is unstinting in His commendation. Those eyes of fire that can single out the false can also discern the genuine. During the Thyatira period the darkness seemed to be impenetrable, but there was a ray of light.

In the days of Elijah, the idolatry in Israel seemed so widespread and the apostasy so general that the situation appeared hopeless. Elijah said, "I, even I only, am left" (1 Kings 19:14). But he was wrong. He was not really left alone. The Lord answered His dispirited prophet, "I have left seven thousand in Israel, all the knees which have not bowed unto Baal" (1 Kings 19:18). Though the entire church age has been marked by opposition of every description, God has never left this earth without His witnesses who love and serve Him. As the present age continues on its course, apostasy and idolatry will increase, but there always will be those who love the Lord and His Word. God will reserve to Himself His true Church. The darker the night the more the devoted and diligent the Lord's faithful ones will shine.

The Condemnation of Thyatira

This is the longest of the seven letters. Most of its content deals with the heresy that had crept into the church at Thyatira. It seems to have revolved around a woman named Jezebel. The Lord said, "Notwithstanding I have a few things against thee, because thou sufferest that woman Jezebel, which calleth herself a prophetess, to teach and to seduce My servants to commit fornication, and to eat things sacrificed unto idols" (Revelation 2:20). The mere mention of that name takes us back to the Old Testament to the wicked wife of King Ahab, the prophetic antitype of the Jezebel in Thyatira. Her father was one of the prophets and priests of Baal, and the whole family seems to have been known for their idolatry, wickedness, and cruelty. There is one Old Testament passage which is strikingly analogous to the Scripture we are considering in Revelation 2. In 2 Kings 9:22 Joram asked Jehu, "Is it peace?" Jehu replied by saying, "What peace, so long as the whoredoms of thy mother Jezebel and her witchcrafts are so many?" This passage sums up the character and influence of that wicked woman. It was she who caused Israel to sin so grievously in committing fornication with the gods of the heathen. Her sorcery and chicanery deceived the people and led them into gross apostasy. There is a correspondence between the Jezebel of the old dispensation and the Jezebel of the church dispensation.

The excellencies in the church at Thyatira were overshadowed by a serious defect. The first person to entice the members of that church into apostasy was a woman. The church was active in love and service and faith, but its members were lying in spiritual adultery. The domineering prophetess had led them astray. The church was a beehive of activity and crowded with people, but it was more like a religious club than a true Christian assembly. The source of the trouble lay with a woman who was religious, but notoriously immoral. She claimed the right to the office of a prophetess, but she persuaded many of the Christians, new converts to Christ, to continue their pagan worship. She was fulfilling the role of the historic Jezebel of the Old Testament. She is the symbol of corruption and idolatry.

Prophetically, the letter to the assembly in Thyatira foreshadows that period in church history known as the Middle Ages. If in the seven churches of Asia Minor we correctly discern a picture of the church from seven different aspects, and covering seven periods of time, the prophetic picture becomes more vivid. The prominent place of a woman prophetess in the church at Thyatira foreshadows the rise of the unscriptural exaltation and worship of Mary. Moreover, the eating of "things sacrificed unto idols" (Revelation 2:20) foreshadows the introduction of the false doctrine of transubstantiation, a basic error of the church in the Middle Ages. The church was characterized by ardent and abundant religious life of the emotional and experiential kind, but the religion was a departure from the objective teaching of the Word of God. The church was weak in doctrine and the knowledge of the Scriptures and therefore took on a mystic tendency.

This marked the beginning of a horrible heresy that gained a strong foothold in the eighth century and has continued to the present. Mary continues to be exalted, idols and images form a part of worship, and the observance of the Lord's Supper is transformed into another sacrifice of Christ. In my judgment this was a degeneration of the most serious nature in the church of Christ. It was introduced by a woman who was mystically inclined, and who was allowed to teach her false doctrine, and that in spite of the fact that a woman was "not ... to teach, nor to usurp authority over the man, but to be in silence" (1 Timothy 2:12). If you are asking, How could this happen? there is but one answer: the little assembly in Thyatira allowed experience to take precedence over the objective standards of God's Word. They were not able to discern the spirits according to 1 John 4:1. How serious was the heresy in Thyatira? Jesus described it as "the depths of Satan" (Revelation 2:24). Of all the women mentioned in the Old Testament none was more deceptive, more daring, more destructive than Jezebel. Her counterpart has carried over into the church age and continues to the present.

The parallel between Christ's fourth parable and His fourth epistle is obvious. The two contain the same basic message. In both a woman introduces an evil which lowered the standard between Christ's own and the world. By the Middle Ages the influence of the leaven was widespread. People who professed to be Christ's followers were playing the harlot with those persons and principles that were opposed to Him. The spirit of worldliness had spread to proportions unprecedented in the Church's history.

That woman who was the instigator of all this evil "calleth herself a prophetess" (2:20). She was a self-appointed, self-styled prophetess. She assumed that title. She was an idolatrous, wicked woman; a prophetess never! The fourth parable and the fourth epistle outline in the clearest possible manner a prophetic preview of the fourth historic phase of the Christian profession. The leading subject in both parable and epistle is identical, the one being complementary and supplementary to the other. Their harmony is not fortuitous but designed. The leaven of an elaborate system of sensual religion merged the whole of Christendom into a state of idolatry, a system the more specious and subtle because it was founded on the name of Jesus Christ. An evil woman succeeded in paganizing the professing church of Christ.

That system remains with us today and it is growing and developing into a huge ecclesiastical system. It is the world church, the ecumenical church reaching out to embrace the whole inhabited earth. It seems to me to be an unfair and unreasonable conclusion to say that these seven letters contain no reference whatever either to prophecy or to the history of the church era. These seven letters are a prominent part of a book which is specifically designated as a book of ''prophecy'' (1:3; 22:18). And the prophecies present indubitable evidence of continuing growth in evil and apostasy. The severity and sharpness of our Lord's words are in themselves proof that He is displeased with what He sees. This is for many professing Christians a sad and startling revelation. It causes dismay to the sincere people who know only a social gospel and who still cherish a hope that the church will save the world. But to the contrary, both prophecy and history, as seen in the seven parables and seven letters, show that the professed church is being converted to the world.

Many are asking, Is there no hope? Is Christ's Church a total failure? My answer is *yes* and *no*. Yes, there is hope. To the question, Is Christ's Church a total failure? my reply is *no*.

To the faithful ones in Thyatira our Lord said, "But that which ye have already hold fast till I come" (2:25). Here is the Christian's assuring hope in our Lord's words, "*till I come.*" The promise of His coming again would motivate the true believers to hold fast to the faith. Those who have been influenced by the leaven of idolatry and wickedness He will judge. The Jezebel form of Christendom must face severe judgment when Christ comes, but to His own He says, "I will come again, and receive you unto Myself; that where I am, there ye may be also" (John 14:3). This is the hope that He left with the little flock in the midst of Thyatira, and it has become the hope of millions since. It is my hope. Is it yours?

We conclude our study of this fourth epistle by drawing attention to some of the correspondences which exist between it and the fourth parable in Matthew 13.

The fourth parable:

The central figure in the parable is the *woman* who hides the leaven in the three measures of meal.

Leaven in the New Testament invariably represents *evil*.

The woman worked *silently*, *stealthily*, and *secretly*.

The whole of the meal was ultimately corrupted by the leaven.

The fourth epistle:

The central figure in this epistle is the *woman* Jezebel.

Jezebel called herself a prophetess and taught *evil* doctrine.

Stealth and *secrecy* characterized the papal system.

There are not lacking signs to show that in the future the whole of Christendom will again be dominated by the world church.

16

THE LETTER TO SARDIS

REPUTATION WITHOUT REALITY

And unto the angel of the church in Sardis write; These things saith He that hath the seven Spirits of God, and the seven stars; I know thy works, that thou hast a name that thou livest, and art dead. Be watchful, and strengthen the things which remain, that are ready to die: for I have not found thy works perfect before God. Remember therefore how thou hast received and heard, and hold fast, and repent. If therefore thou shalt not watch, I will come on thee as a thief, and thou shalt not know what hour I will come upon thee. Thou hast a few names even in Sardis which have not defiled their garments; and they shall walk with Me in white: for they are worthy. He that overcometh, the same shall be clothed in white raiment; and I will not blot out his name out of the book of life, but I will confess his name before My Father, and before His angels. He that hath an ear, let him hear what the Spirit saith unto the churches (Revelation 3:1-6).

The fifth letter in our Lord's series of seven was addressed to the church at Sardis. The city lay about twenty-eight miles south of Thyatira. In ancient days it was a prominent and wealthy city, the capital of the kingdom of Lydia. Its success and fame lasted for about two thousand years. Like most of the other cities mentioned in these seven church messages, Sardis passed into obscurity.

The word Sardis, according to some expositors, proposes a Hebrew derivation from the word *sahrad*, which means "to escape," which in its noun form would signify the escaping ones, or those who come out. If this interpretation of the word is warranted, it throws some light upon the next period in church history. It was the Reformation era, the period of the Renaissance, which continued from about A.D. 1500 to 1750.

In our study of the parables we noted a distinct break between the first four and the three which followed. When our Lord completed the fourth parable, that of the leaven, He dismissed the multitudes and went into the house, where His disciples followed Him. The last three parables were spoken in private to the disciples.

When we come to the message to Sardis there is a break. The progress of evil seems to have ceased. Now I did not say that evil ceased, but that its *progress* did. In Thyatira Christ saw "the depths of Satan," and that is as far as evil can go. Nothing can go beyond "the depths of Satan." In the letter to Sardis there is a new direction, a new course of flow in religious thought. For nine centuries, during the Thyatira period, there was a rapid ripening of human corruptions within Christendom. Images were worshiped, relics were adored, sinners were immortalized as saints, and mortal men professed to possess a divine power to localize the Lord Jesus Christ upon an earthly altar. For centuries it seemed that Satan's reign over Christendom would never end. The triumph of the serpent seemed complete. Hundreds of millions were duped into believing that Satan's church was the true church.

But Satan's plans were to meet with resistance. In the fifteenth century, when the outlook of the church was the darkest, when the gloom of that long night was the deepest, the morning of deliverance broke. Christ's little flock knew what He meant when He said, "Lo, I am with you alway, even unto the end of the [age]." The Lord's remnant, the little company of the elect, was to rise up. The Reformation was about to be born. A little company of the elect refused to bow the knee to Baal. Not since the day of Pentecost had there been such a display of human courage and such a manifestation of the Spirit's power.

One of the secrets of Satan's success lay in the fact that the Holy Scriptures were withheld from the people. The organized church was given priority over the Bible. For centuries the Scriptures had lain silent in dead languages. This was Satan's masterpiece of strategy for he knew the power of the Word of God. In his confrontation with Christ in the wilderness he felt the power of the sword of the Spirit each time our Lord quoted the Scriptures. Satan would never forget that sword thrust, "It is written."

We are perhaps now in the position to appreciate the meaning and significance of the name Sardis. If the Hebrew derivation is correct, and Sardis means *the escaping ones*, we have an indication of the immediate results of the Reformation. As the result of the work of the Reformers there was a literal escape of Protestants from the tyrannical bondage of Rome. Those who were delivered from that yoke might aptly be designated the escaping ones.

One of the key factors of the Protestant Reformation was the invention of the printing press. The human instrument in God's hands was Johann Gutenberg of Germany. The first press was completed in the middle of the sixteenth century and the first book to come from that press was the Bible. Hidden truths were rediscovered and unbiblical practices of the church were exposed. Luther, Zwingli, Calvin, and others were the leaders of the Reformation that swept over Europe.

But the Reformation fell short of accomplishing much that might have been achieved. What appeared to be a mighty advance in the first decades of the Reformation was short-lived. We are thankful for what was accomplished after Martin Luther nailed his ninety-five theses on the church door at Wittenburg, Germany, on October 31, 1517 A.D. I am not finding fault with the Augsburg Confession, the Heidelburg Confession, or the Westminster Confession. But something went wrong. What really happened? We can find some answers in our Lord's letter to the church at Sardis.

The Church That Was Popular

Our Lord said, "Thou hast a name that thou livest" (3:1). Sardis had the church with a "name." It was the church with a reputation. It was well attended and well advertised with a reputation for being alive. It was known as *the church which is alive*.

At one time Sardis was one of the greatest and most attractive cities in the world. The empire over which the king of Lydia ruled was known for its oriental splendor and far-reaching influence. The wealth, magnificence, and luxury of Sardis were unsurpassed. There was hardly a day when the city did not teem with life.

William Barclay writes how "Solon, the wisest of the Greeks, came on a visit to Sardis. He was shown the wealth, the splendor, the luxury. He saw also the blind confidence of King Croesus and his people that nothing could end this splendor; but he also saw that the seeds of softness, of flabbiness, and of inevitable degeneration were being sown. And it was then that Solon uttered his famous saying to Croesus, 'Call no man happy until he is dead.' The wise Greek knew only too well the chances and the changes of life which Croesus had forgotten.''

When John penned this letter to Sardis the change had already taken place. The once famous capital had been reduced to a monument. Sardis had been defeated militarily and had degenerated morally. The city had a reputation for life but it was dead. I have visited places in our own United States that were like that. Maps and tourist guides invite you to come and see those famous historic sites. But some of them are mere ghost towns. They are still popular tourist attractions, but the things that made them famous are gone. They have a name, but they are dead.

The Sardis-type church is with us today. I have preached in some of them. They have a good name. They have a wide reputation. They offer an adequate bus service for transporting people to and from the church. They baptize people and turn in good reports. They boast large numbers, but some of them are dead. They are teeming with activity, are well informed and orthodox, but waning in spiritual power.

The Reformation brought religious freedom, but before the enthusiasm of victory had passed away, the Protestants themselves began to turn against each other, the outcome of which was the formation of themselves into antagonistic denominations and sects. Religion began to be viewed from a merely intellectual standpoint. The Reformation began well, and some of its beneficent effects are still with us, yet reluctantly we are compelled to acknowledge that the movement has long since ceased to be an active power. The noble work begun by its founders has not been followed up by their successors. Someone has said, "Go throughout Christendom, and you will find the gospel in a coffin."

The Church That Was Powerless

The character in which our Lord addresses Himself to this church is strikingly appropriate and pertinent to its condition. "These things saith He that hath the seven Spirits" (Revelation 3:1). This descriptive term, *the seven Spirits of God*, takes us back to the first chapter which speaks of "the seven Spirits ... before His throne" (1:4). The phrase appears again with a direct reference to the seven eyes (5:6). Seven being the number of completion or perfection, I take this phrase to indicate the Holy Spirit in the fullness of His wisdom and power.

There is an allusion to this in Isaiah 11:2-3, which seems to fit into our Lord's complaint: "Thou hast a name that thou livest, and art dead" (Revelation 3:1). Of course He meant that the church was spiritually dead. The church had everything to glorify itself in the eyes of the world but nothing that glorified God. In that one brief, swift sentence, *thou art dead*, He revealed the church's lack. The church at Sardis was popular but powerless. There was no evidence of the Holy Spirit's presence nor His power.

The church had a reputation that it was living, but it did not live up to this reputation. A dead church presents a most miserable picture.

This letter to the church at Sardis speaks a solemn word to all who have ears to hear. The ecclesiastical order in many churches is being maintained without the slightest semblance of the Spirit's presence and power. Many churches could carry on with the success and popularity they are now enjoying even if the Holy Spirit were not in existence. They have the reputation of being alive but they are dead. They have fallen into a deep spiritual slumber. They are making no spiritual impact whatever. This is a picture of Christendom today. Just as our Lord predicted in the parables, the world, the flesh, and the devil are militating against the Word of God, the tares are mixed with the wheat, and the spreading mustard tree continues to attract buzzards in its branches.

Now it is of prime importance that we bear in mind that this condition of Christian profession is to continue until the end of the age. Each of the seven churches had in them certain characteristics which will continue to develop until the time when the Lord finally spues out of His mouth (rejects) the apostate church (3:16). Protestantism today is an effete power and a spent force. Surely the most optimistic among us cannot deny that the Protestantism of the last three hundred and fifty years, with its confidence in human scholarship and intellectualism, has not yielded to the Person and power of the Holy Spirit. The enormous toleration which is shown to Satan's growing ecumenical church is alarming, to say the least.

How different are the Lord's judgments to man's! The

ecclesiastical and religious world regards Sardis as a live church but the Lord says she is dead. Smyrna was despised on account of her material poverty and lack of this world's goods, yet the Lord said, "Thou art rich" (2:9). The church at Laodicea boasted saying, "I am rich," but the Lord said, "Thou art ... poor" (3:17). The condition of the Laodicean church is reflected in our own times. Our churches need to reflect on the words of Jehovah who said, "For My thoughts are not your thoughts, neither are your ways My ways, saith the LORD. For as the heavens are higher than the earth, so are My ways higher than your ways, and My thoughts than your thoughts" (Isaiah 55:8-9). Truly "the LORD seeth not as man seeth; for man looketh on the outward appearance, but the LORD looketh on the heart" (1 Samuel 16:7). Many Protestant churches are allied to a system and are gathered to a name which is powerless and lifeless. The appearance of life and the proud claims do not deceive Him who is omniscient and in uncompromising language says, "Thou ... art dead."

Three hundred years ago the Reformation forces looked as though they might sheer the enemy of his power. But as Christ taught in the parables, and as history shows, the final victory was not to be realized until the King returns. The words addressed to the church at Sardis apply prophetically to Christendom. The churches are waning in spiritual power and are defective in quality because the personality of the Holy Spirit and His relation to the Church in general and to individual believers in particular are subjects which are but dimly comprehended. The Sardian condition in Christendom is proof that the Holy

Spirit is not controlling the hearts of the people. The word of the Lord to Zerubbabel needed to be stressed in Sardis: "Not by might, nor by power, but by My Spirit, saith the LORD of hosts" (Zechariah 4:6).

Sin, in one or more of its various forms, had gotten into the church at Sardis. The Scriptures frequently associate death with sin. As a matter of fact, sin and death are never disassociated. Jeremiah wrote, "But every one shall die for his own iniquity" (Jeremiah 31:30). Ezekiel added, "The soul that sinneth, it shall die" (Ezekiel 18:4). Christians who are yielded to God are "as those that are alive from the dead" (Romans 6:13). To that Paul added, "The wages of sin is death" (Romans 6:23). He wrote further that Christians, in their preconverted days, "were dead in trespasses and sins" (Ephesians 2:1,5). In one of the pastoral Epistles we are reminded that "She that liveth in pleasure is dead while she liveth" (1 Timothy 5:6). James wrote, "Sin, when it is finished, bringeth forth death" (James 1:15). We are not told precisely which sin, or sins, entered the church at Sardis, but we do know that a kind of death overtook the pastor and the people. It was the church "having a form of godliness, but denying the power thereof" (2 Timothy 3:5). The *form* was present but the *force* was gone. The Lord Jesus called it a dead church. What a pity!

The Church With a Prospect

To the Sardian church, which applies prophetically to Protestantism, our Lord said, "Be watchful, and strengthen the things which remain" (Revelation 3:2).

Here is a word the church needed to heed for, continues the Lord, "[They] are ready to die." There was still a spark of life. "Thou hast a few names even in Sardis which have not defiled their garments" (3:4). There was still a pulse beat. Life was not totally extinct. The saints in Sardis were few and sickly, but apparently our Lord saw that hope had not died completely. The "few" offered some prospect for the future.

We may see, therefore, in view of Christ's words, that even though the church in Sardis was in a miserable condition, the situation was not hopeless. The few who were not completely devoid of spiritual life might still repent and be changed. They must remember what they had "received and heard, and hold fast, and repent" (3:3). The reference is, of course, to the pure gospel of justification by the free grace of faith. It was that truth for which the Reformers stood, a truth that to this day is slowly disappearing from our midst. The total ruin and corruption of man, which supplies the necessity for divine regeneration and justification, is belittled from many pulpits; it would follow logically that we do not need the blood of Christ for the remission of our sins. Thus there is a need that the *few* should "strengthen the things that remain."

The few are the minority in the parable of the sower "that received seed into the good ground" (Matthew 13:23), they are the children of the kingdom in the parable of the tares (Matthew 13:38). They are the faithful few in whom there is a ray of hope until the King returns. The buzzards in the branches of the mustard tree will increase in number, and the leaven of evil will continue its work, but the Lord's few will continue until He returns. He said, "I will build My church; and the gates of hell shall not prevail against it" (Matthew 16:18). Christ's Church is not organized religion, it is not denominationalism, it is not the World Council of Churches. Christ's Church is an organism consisting of those who have been born again. The ministry of the few is that of continuing to sow the seed of God's Word.

Those who have chosen to identify themselves with the Lord Jesus Christ never were in the majority. Our Lord said, "Enter ye in at the strait gate: for wide is the gate, and broad is the way, that leadeth to destruction, and *many* there be which go in thereat: Because strait is the gate, and narrow is the way, which leadeth unto life, and *few* there be that find it" (Matthew 7:13-14). Our Lord's two terms, the "many" and the "few," suggest the twofold division of the human race. The way of the few is the narrow way, but it leads at last to life in its highest form. The few are the Master's minority.

If souls are to be rescued from the ruin of the Sardian situation, the few must "be watchful" (Revelation 3:2). "Now it is high time to awake out of sleep" (Romans 13:11). "Watch ye, stand fast in the faith, quit you like men, be strong" (1 Corinthians 16:13). "Therefore let us not sleep, as do others; but let us watch and be sober" (1 Thessalonians 5:6). "Watch and pray, that ye enter not into temptation" (Matthew 26:41). "Be sober, be vigilant; because your adversary the devil, as a roaring lion, walketh about, seeking whom he may devour" (1 Peter 5:8). "Therefore watch" (Acts 20:31). The Christian must make certain that every day is a Watch Day.

Like the church in Sardis, many a church in our day has fallen asleep. They have a name that they live, but are dead. We need to salvage the saints, gather together our gifts and our goods, and by prompt action get on with the sowing of the seed of God's Word. Christ's message to the church of the first century is needed in the churches in every century.

Of the five letters we have examined so far, the Sardian epistle is the only one in which there is no reference made to assailants. In each of the first four we are told there was some menacing foe either within or without, who was leading the saints astray or else corrupting the pure Word of God. But in Sardis Satan stayed in the background. Have you ever wondered why? I will tell you why. Satan never troubles a sleeping church. He is afraid he might waken it. In their false security he lets them sleep. Christians, beware! It is high time to awake out of our slumber.

17

THE LETTER TO PHILADELPHIA

FEEBLE BUT FAITHFUL

*And to the angel of the church in Philadelphia write;
These things saith He that is holy, He that is true, He that
hath the key of David, He that openeth, and no man
shutteth; and shutteth, and no man openeth; I know thy
works: behold, I have set before thee an open door, and no
man can shut it: for thou hast a little strength, and hast kept
My word, and hast not denied My name. Behold, I will make
them of the synagogue of Satan, which say they are Jews, and
are not, but do lie; behold, I will make them to come and
worship before thy feet, and to know that I have loved thee.
Because thou hast kept the word of My patience, I also will
keep thee from the hour of temptation, which shall come
upon all the world, to try them that dwell upon the earth.
Behold, I come quickly: hold that fast which thou hast, that
no man take thy crown. Him that overcometh will I make a
pillar in the temple of My God, and he shall go no more out:
and I will write upon him the name of My God, and the
name of the city of My God, which is new Jerusalem, which
cometh down out of heaven from My God: and I will write
upon him My new name. He that hath an ear, let him hear
what the Spirit saith unto the churches (Revelation 3:7-13).*

Of the seven letters addressed to the churches in Asia
Minor, there were but two of them that received no
rebuke—the congregations of Smyrna and Philadelphia.
The latter is the subject of our discussion in this present

chapter. These two churches had something in common. Both churches were insignificant in the eyes of the world, small, poor, and of little strength. Both had to contend with the same enemies, a segment of Jews who were of "the synagogue of Satan" (Revelation 2:9; 3:9).

Philadelphia was situated about thirty miles southeast of Sardis. It was founded about 200 B.C. by Attalus Philadelphus. *Philadelphia* is the Greek word for brotherly love or one who loves his brother. The word appears not less than seven times in the New Testament (Romans 12:10; 1 Thessalonians 4:9; Hebrews 13:1; 1 Peter 1:22; 2 Peter 1:7; Revelation 3:7). This last appearance is the only reference to the city.

In my comments on the messages to the churches I have tried to show that, in addition to their *primary association* with the churches then in existence, they have in them a *prophetic anticipation*, a preview of the entire church age leading to Christ's return. As we look back on church history, the period described in the epistle to Philadelphia is the post-Reformation era commencing about A.D. 1750 to approximately 1900 or even a little later, a time within the memory of persons living today. Following the period of the Reformation the true Church shone forth as a beacon light in a new way. She heeded the Lord's exhortation to Sardis to "Be watchful, and strengthen the things which remain, that are ready to die" (3:2).

The Lord describes her as a church with "little strength." It is Christ's description of her condition outwardly as compared with the strength of the world. It was comparatively small in numbers, and poor financially. It could not count among its members the rich and influential of the world. What our Lord said about the church in Philadelphia could be said of other churches. However, of the church in Philadelphia this was especially true. In that one short phrase we have a description of the church from the external viewpoint. The Philadelphian churches today would no doubt be advised to merge with some other church as soon as possible.

It must be said with emphasis that the description of the church at Philadelphia outwardly did not apply to her true spiritual condition. Spiritually, the little flock in Philadelphia was not without strength, but to the contrary they were quite strong. Our Lord revealed the secret of that church's spiritual strength when He said, "Thou ... hast kept My word" (3:8). Keeping the Word of the Lord does not mean that they merely believed it. There are professing Christians in dead churches who will tell you they believe God's Word, but their belief is merely intellectual and academic. They hold to a dead orthodoxy of the letter without the Spirit. It is a kind of belief which is elsewhere condemned in Scripture (Romans 2:29), and which demons themselves possess (James 2:19).

The church in Philadelphia guarded the integrity of God's Word by their behavior. They were not mere hearers of the Word but doers as well (James 1:22). Paul wrote, "For not the hearers of the law are just before God, but the doers of the law shall be justified" (Romans 2:13). The keeping of God's Word will provide the necessary strength for any individual or any church. The Apostle John wrote, "I have written unto you, young men, because ye are strong, and the Word of God abideth in you, and ye have overcome the wicked one" (1 John 2:14).

Joshua said, "This book of the law shall not depart out of thy mouth; but thou shalt meditate therein day and night, that thou mayest observe to do according to all that is written therein: for then thou shalt make thy way prosperous, and then thou shalt have good success" (Joshua 1:8). In Philadelphia the world looked upon a little flock with little strength, but the little flock was strong in God's Word.

Today we are being asked to abandon the Scriptures to "science falsely so called" (1 Timothy 6:20); salvation through the redeeming work of Christ to modern psychiatry; the preaching and teaching of God's Word to psychology counselors, seminars, feminars, and discussion groups. The church in Philadelphia, however, is commended for keeping the Word of the Lord. They remained faithful to the truth of the gospel. That is the key to success in Christian life and service. Fidelity to the Word of the Lord is a divine imperative. When an individual or a church wavers in loyalty to God's Word, spiritual strength must wane. Philadelphia had that great quality and characteristic of being faithful to the Word of the Lord, being in complete subjection to the whole of the Holy Scriptures. The sophistries of higher critics and the half-truths of a rationalistic philosophy could not weaken their confidence in the written revelation of God.

Loyalty to the Scriptures was not the only strong point in the church at Philadelphia. The Lord continued, "Thou ... hast not denied My name" (Revelation 3:8). They had not merely made a confession of their faith in Christ, but theirs was a manifested loyalty to Christ Himself. They had only a little strength as man reckons strength, but their divine resources enabled them to remain faithful to the One who had redeemed them. They did not nor could not remain quiet about the name of their wonderful Lord and Saviour. The person who is loyal to the Scriptures will be loyal to the Christ of the Scriptures. The name of Christ represents Christ Himself, His deity, holiness, righteousness, glory, sovereignty, eternality. Wherever the name of the Lord Jesus Christ is magnified and glorified there is blessing and power. We are not surprised, therefore, when the Lord announces to this church the open door.

The Open Door

He said, "I have set before thee an open door" (3:8). What did the Lord mean by the use of this figurative expression? If we rely upon other Scripture portions, thereby comparing spiritual things with spiritual, the meaning can hardly be dubious. Paul used this expression on a number of occasions. In every instance the open door has reference to an opportunity created by the Lord for the preaching of the gospel of Christ. It was the open door of missionary opportunity.

Luke tells how Paul, at the end of his first missionary campaign, returned to Antioch. The church at Antioch had commended Paul and Barnabas to the grace of God and sent them on their way. The believers at Antioch were now waiting expectantly for a report from Paul. Will he tell them how he was beaten and stoned? Will he show them the bruises and scars on his body? Listen to his testimony: "And when they were come, and had gathered the church together, they rehearsed all that God had done with them, and how He had opened the door of faith unto the Gentiles'' (Acts 14:27). His report was a testimony of praise to God who had "opened the door."

Paul used the figure of the open door to tell the believers in Corinth why he must remain a while at Ephesus. "But I will tarry at Ephesus until Pentecost. For a great door and effectual is opened unto me, and there are many adversaries" (1 Corinthians 16:8-9). There were two reasons for his remaining at Ephesus; the open door of opportunity to witness for Christ, and the open opposition of the enemies of the gospel. In Ephesus there was the pressure of the heathen worshipers of Diana who were prostituting their religion for gain. But God had opened the door of service for Paul and the enemy could not close it.

When Paul wrote to the Christians at Colosse he asked his friends to pray for him "that God would open unto us a door of utterance, to speak the mystery of Christ, for which I am also in bonds" (Colossians 4:3). Paul had the unfortunate experience of pushing open a door that God had to shut. Luke wrote how Paul was "forbidden of the Holy Ghost to preach the word in Asia" (Acts 16:6), and how "they assayed to go into Bithynia: but the Spirit suffered them not" (verse 7). Thus Paul was able to write, "Furthermore, when I came to Troas to preach Christ's gospel, and a door was opened unto me of the Lord" (2 Corinthians 2:12). The great apostle learned that it was better to pray than push. Note carefully the burden of Paul's prayer request. He was not asking selfishly, but that God would open a door of utterance. He had learned that when God opens a door, neither man nor devil can shut it.

The meaning of the open door in the letter to the church at Philadelphia therefore is obviously that the Lord Himself would create an opportunity for the preaching of the gospel, a door of missionary opportunity. Their material resources and numerical strength might be small, but their opportunity for service was large. We may conclude that if the Lord opened the door for a greater outreach with His gospel, then the church in Philadelphia was prepared to walk through that door. That church was characterized by vision, compassion, and zeal, and now the Lord opened a door so widely that no force on earth or in hell could close it.

The open door extended to the church in Philadelphia is a challenge to the churches in our day. In this generation bigness is counted an indication of blessing, wealth to some suggests worthfulness. But the devil's crowd is not few in number, neither are they poor. Now I am not suggesting that God puts a premium on poverty and smallness. Not at all! But too frequently the big talk of the day is of money, men, and methods; baptisms, buildings, and busses. I am not opposing all these. We ought to enlist the best men, and employ the soundest methods, and encourage the giving of money, all of which are essential if we are going to do the best job possible for God. But I fear that sometimes the dependence is more upon these things than upon Him who opens and shuts doors.

Let the church of today remember that she is in herself of little strength, and that the Lord is able to manifest His strength in human weakness. Let us never forget that

"God hath chosen the weak things of the world to confound the things which are mighty" (1 Corinthians 1:27). When Paul recognized his weakness, when he was conscious of it, then he was in a state best suited for God to demonstrate His power through him. The apostle wrote, "When I am weak, then am I strong" (2 Corinthians 12:10). Paul's weakness was not self-inflicted, it was not the consequence of his own folly, it was the result of his sufferings *for Christ's sake*. It was said of Paul, "His bodily presence is weak" (2 Corinthians 10:10), but it was to that man that the Lord opened many doors.

In the church in Philadelphia we see smallness and weakness as viewed through the eyes of man. Yet the Lord said, "I have set before thee an open door, and no man can shut it." As we look back into church history we can see in Christ's words a great prophecy that had its fulfillment in the eighteenth and nineteenth centuries. It was the period of the *open door*, a time in the history of Christianity when there was a strong emphasis on the study of the Bible, a return to the fundamentals of the faith, and a revival of the Church's *blessed hope* in the return of the Lord Jesus Christ. There appears to be much in Christ's prophecy and its fulfillment in Christian profession which corresponds to Philadelphia.

The Obvious Developments

Before we examine some obvious developments during the Philadelphian era, let us glance back beyond the nineteenth century. Was the Reformation the work of God or was it the work of men? Was it a movement of the Holy Spirit or the efforts of the flesh? My own feelings in the matter are that the work of the Reformers was directed of the Holy Spirit. However, I will hasten to add that the effort of the Reformers' *successors* was a fleshly or human effort, and that in time it was devoid of real spiritual life and power. Worship became cold, formal, and lifeless.

There was a bright spot however when, for several generations, the efforts of John and Charles Wesley accomplished much for the cause of Christ in Great Britain. Once again the gospel of the grace of God was clearly sounded forth and the foundation doctrine of justification by faith was insisted upon. Many unlettered but Spirit-filled men went about the country pointing others to the Lamb of God. Many were saved and gathered together regularly to study God's Word and to strengthen and edify one another. Class meetings were formed and love feasts were held where brotherly love prevailed. But it did not take the devil long to recover from the blow dealt to him. He succeeded in leading the followers of Wesley to make the same mistake as did the successors of Luther. A human organization was formed, a man was unduly exalted, and a human name was magnified and well-nigh deified. The followers of Wesley were no longer contented to be known as "Christians," but instead adopted the title of "Methodists" with which the world has since dubbed them. Later they preferred to be known as "Wesleyans." The Bible as the final authority for belief and behavior was supplanted by the "society rules." Wesley's fifty-three sermons, designed to meet the needs of his preachers, were required reading for all who sought to enter the "Methodist ministry." One young man, desiring to become a Wesleyan Methodist "local preacher," was examined by the superintendent of the circuit in which he then resided. He was asked if he had read Wesley's *Notes on the New Testament*, Wesley's *Catechism*, and Wesley's *Fifty-three Sermons*. But he was not asked whether he had read the Holy Scriptures. Many followers of Wesley had fallen into the same net which ensnared the successors of the Reformers.

One day our Lord said to Peter, "I will build My Church; and the gates of hell shall not prevail against it" (Matthew 16:18). And now He is conveying to the church at Philadelphia the same basic idea in His words, "I have set before thee an open door, and no man can shut it" (Revelation 3:8). In Philadelphia a door was opened by Christ. Not that the task for those believers was to be an easy one. As Paul found it in Ephesus so the Christians would discover it in Philadelphia. There would be "many adversaries" (1 Corinthians 16:9). As we noted earlier in the study, a segment of the Jewish population in Philadelphia was displaying a fanatical resistance to the gospel of their Messiah. Christ referred to them as being of "the synagogue of Satan, which say they are Jews, and are not" (Revelation 3:9). The Philadelphian Christians would not have an easy time of it. In the very city where Jewish antagonism was running high the Lord opened a door for the gospel. If the professing Christians in Philadelphia had truly gone in through the door of salvation they would now go out through the door of service. Jesus said, "I am the door: by Me if any man enter in, he shall be saved, and shall go in and out, and find pasture" (John 10:9). There you have it! In for salvation, out for service.

The prophetic anticipation in our Lord's letter to the Philadelphian church was fulfilled in the eighteenth and nineteenth centuries. It should be stated here, and with emphasis, that the full application of the prophetic burden in the Philadelphian message cannot be limited to any one person nor to any one single historical fulfillment. There were many men and movements which took advantage of the "open door." There is not a single man or movement that can lay an exclusive claim to be the church of Philadelphia. In smaller or greater measure every spiritual awakening which is the result of the work of the Holy Spirit, regardless of the person or organization used of God, is to some degree the antitype to Philadelphia. The Christian church will long remember such names as George Whitfield, William Carey, John and Charles Wesley, Adoniram Judson, Charles Finney, John Charles Ryle, D.L. Moody, Billy Sunday, Wilbur Chapman, R.A. Torrey, and many others.

In my consideration of the prophetic import of the Philadelphian message I cannot exclude a movement which had its origin in Dublin, Ireland. I am thinking of the movement which has come to be known as "Brethrenism" or, as it has been erroneously called, "Plymouth Brethren." The origin of this movement was the simple desire on the part of a few of the Lord's people to know more of Him and His Word. From a study of the Scriptures they came to the conclusion that it was not necessary for an ordained minister to preach God's Word and administer the Lord's Supper, but all believers share in common this privilege. Accordingly, believers in Christ gathered together to remember the Lord's death in the "breaking of bread" without the assistance of any so-called ecclesiastic. No distinction was made between clergy and laity. The movement was, as all movements are which are energized by the Holy Spirit, without display, ostentation, worldly pomp, or show. They freely recognized the common brotherhood of all the born-again ones. This quiet and unobtrusive yet influential movement was greatly used of God during that open-door period of the eighteenth and nineteenth centuries.

The promise of the open door to the church at Philadelphia is highly significant when we remember that prophetically it brings us to the time of the end. When rightly understood by the Lord's people it cannot fail to be a stimulus to their faith and a spur to their zeal. Yes, prophetically the open door has reference to God's last witness and appeal to an evil and apostate world in this dispensation. Before Enoch was removed from the antedeluvian world, he proclaimed the impending judgment of God. Before the flood came upon the earth and destroyed the godless and wicked sinners, Noah was sent as a preacher of righteousness to warn them of the coming disaster. Before the angel of death destroyed all the firstborn in Egypt, Moses and Aaron were sent to Pharaoh entreating him to relent and heed the commands of God. Before Titus besieged Jerusalem, pillaged the city, and scattered the inhabitants, the Lord Jesus warned the nation of Israel of coming judgment. And before Christ comes to take His own to be with Himself He has opened the door and given an opportunity for the preaching and hearing of the gospel as never before, and for the proclamation of His imminent return. It is His final appeal, His last witness to sinners.

The pearl in the sixth parable is the Church. The principle message in the sixth letter speaks prophetically of the Church's last opportunity to take the gospel to the uttermost part of the earth. The door remains open as of this present hour. How long before our Lord comes again and closes the door of service for His Church none of us know. The Christian life is a life of give and take. Our Lord said, "Freely ye have received, freely give" (Matthew 10:8). First we accept what He offers; then we offer what He asks. Have *you* gone through the open door? What portion of *your* time, talents, and treasure are you giving to Christ for the sending forth of the good news of salvation? The door of Christian service is ever and always open, and it will remain open until the end of the dispensation of grace. The greatest rewards that will ever come to any church or individual Christian will be given by Christ according to faithfulness and loyalty and the full use of all that has been entrusted. The church in Philadelphia was feeble but faithful.

The ministry to which God has called me involves about sixty thousand miles of travel and not less than five hundred spoken messages every year. I have preached in more than twelve hundred churches in our country. In my travels I have been an observer. Christians complain that they are not receiving spiritual food from the pulpit. There is little to nourish the soul and satisfy the inner man. People in some churches are being fed with husks. Political and social problems, scientific hypotheses, ethical dissertations, and philosophical ramifications may inform, but they provide no food for the spiritual life. Musical entertainment has a far greater attraction than does the sermon.

Then there are those churches, fewer in number (but we thank God for them), where the Philadelphian spirit is in evidence. The Word of God is being expounded faithfully, Christians have pledged themselves to seek God's will and to prepare for Christian service to go anywhere God may call them. One longs for many more of such Philadelphian churches throughout the world.

18

THE LETTER TO LAODICEA

WEALTHY BUT WANTING

*And unto the angel of the church of the Laodiceans write;
These things saith the Amen, the faithful and true witness,
the beginning of the creation of God; I know thy works, that
thou art neither cold nor hot: I would thou wert cold or hot.
So then because thou art lukewarm, and neither cold nor hot,
I will spue thee out of My mouth. Because thou sayest, I am
rich, and increased with goods, and have need of nothing;
and knowest not that thou art wretched, and miserable, and
poor, and blind, and naked: I counsel thee to buy of Me gold
tried in the fire, that thou mayest be rich; and white raiment,
that thou mayest be clothed, and that the shame of thy
nakedness do not appear; and anoint thine eyes with
eyesalve, that thou mayest see. As many as I love, I rebuke
and chasten: be zealous therefore, and repent. Behold, I
stand at the door, and knock: if any man hear My voice, and
open the door, I will come in to him, and will sup with him,
and he with Me. To him that overcometh will I grant to sit
with Me in My throne, even as I also overcame, and am set
down with My Father in His throne. He that hath an ear, let
him hear what the Spirit saith unto the churches (Revelation
3:14-22).*

Laodicea is the last of the seven churches to receive a
letter from our Lord. In some respects this last letter is the
saddest of them all. In the first six epistles there is to be
found a commendable and an encouraging word. Here

Christ has nothing good to say, only a strong denunciation of complacency.

The city was strategically located in the Lycus Valley about forty-five miles southeast of Philadelphia. Its geographical location contributed greatly to its fame and prosperity. Laodicea was a highly successful financial and commercial center. The remains of temples, theaters, elaborate baths, and the marks of commercial enterprise all give some indication of its former greatness. Reportedly it was one of the wealthiest cities in the world. Pride, luxury, and smugness were the features of the social life in Laodicea.

Laodicea was one of the churches for which Paul expressed great concern. In his Epistle to the neighboring city of Colosse he said, "For I would that ye knew what great conflict I have for you, and for them at Laodicea" (Colossians 2:1). Then at the close of the Colossian Epistle he urged that it be read in the church of the Laodiceans (Colossians 4:16). That was at least twenty-five years before the book of the Revelation was written, so it most assuredly appears that, at the time Paul wrote to the Colossians, the seeds of corruption had already been sown in the church at Laodicea.

God completes His work in cycles of seven. The seven churches combined present seven stages in the life of the church on earth, commencing at Pentecost and concluding with the Rapture at the appearing of Christ. Here then we have a prophetic foreview of the entire church dispensation. The Laodicean letter, which is the last in our Lord's series of seven, brings to a close His own presentation of the church's history on earth. The tares continue to increase among the wheat, buzzards continue to gather in the tree of Christendom, and the leaven of evil is gaining momentum. The church at Laodicea is the church of the end times and it depicts conditions in Christendom when our Lord comes again. What is the church like when Christ returns? Christ tells us plainly in this closing letter. Conditions are more deplorable than at any time in the church's history.

As I study this last letter, I could wish that the letter to the church at Philadelphia had been the last one. But we must deal with the facts as our Lord presented them, and we must face conditions as we find them. We must not indulge in sentiment as we consider the final phase of Christian profession. This study is concerned with the character of professing Christianity during the closing moments of this dispensation of grace and sets forth the woeful state of its spiritual life, a condition that is utterly abhorrent to our Lord.

The meaning of the word *Laodicea* leaves us in no doubt as to the general character of the church which bears its name. Also, we find in the very name of that church an unerring index to the prophetic import of its message. *Laodicea* means ''the rights of the people'' or ''the judgments of the people,'' the general idea being that the masses of the people are asserting themselves and demonstrating their power as never before.

The voice of the people is being heard as never before. Shortly after World War I, in 1920 to be exact, the late Dr. H.A. Ironside said, ''In the great war we were told that our soldiers were fighting to make the world safe *for* democracy. In a little while statesmen will be attempting to raise armies to make the world safe *from* democracy." The day predicted by Dr. Ironside has fallen upon us. The uprising of the masses is being witnessed in almost every country on the earth. Both world governments and the church are being strongly influenced by the will of the people. No longer is the Word of God a lamp for the church's feet and a light for her path. The church is no longer directed by the Head from Heaven, but is governed by the will of the people upon the earth.

I have selected four pertinent points from the Laodicean letter that to me seem appropos.

The Description Christ Stated

It has been pointed out earlier in our study that the descriptive titles and terms used by our Lord in the presentation of Himself to the various churches are appropriate in each case. Certainly this is true in the present letter to the church at Laodicea.

Christ first introduces Himself as the "Amen" (Revelation 3:14). The word literally means *truth*, signifying that which is stable, true, and unchanging. It is divine certainty in contradistinction to human uncertainty. A rationalistic philosophy had undermined the faith of many in the assembly at Laodicea. So here Christ presents Himself as the *Amen*, meaning that He Himself is "the Truth" (John 14:6), who is utterly to be relied upon and unquestionably accepted.

The Hebrew word translated *Amen* is an "adverb of assent," denoting a confirmation of something said or about to be said. At times it appears at the beginning of a statement as in the twenty-five times our Lord used it in the Gospel according to John. There it is translated "verily." When He used the double "verily" He was actually saying "Amen, Amen," or "It is true, it is true." (See John 1:51; 3:3,5,11; 5:19,24,25; 6:26,32,47,53; 8:34,51,58; 10:1,7; 12:24; 13:16,20-21,38; 14:12; 16:20,23; 21:18.)

But here in the Laodicean letter He is not merely saying Amen, but that He Himself is the Amen. He is the very embodiment of truth. The church in Laodicea had departed from Christ, and now its members had their faith undermined and were being tossed to and fro with every wind of doctrine.

Jesus Christ is the Amen One, the only person whose words are true beyond all doubt. His ministry of words and deeds fulfills every promise of God, "For all the promises of God in Him are yea, and in Him Amen" (2 Corinthians 1:20). Thus He presents Himself to the Laodicean assembly as the God of all truth. He said to Pilate, "To this end was I born, and for this cause came I into the world, that I should bear witness unto the truth. Every one that is of the truth heareth My voice" (John 18:37). "All the fullness of the Godhead" dwelt in Him (Colossians 2:9), so what He speaks is honest, accurate, exact. "Never man spake like this man" (John 7:46). "He taught them as one having authority" (Matthew 7:29). He told the Laodicean church that He is "the faithful and true witness" (Revelation 3:14). The Amen is the conclusion because Christ is the finality of truth. The latter phrase, "the faithful and true witness" is an explanation of the name *Amen*. In Laodicea faithful witnesses to the truth of

God were becoming fewer and fewer, and so our Lord's revelation of Himself as "the Amen, the faithful and true witness" is in harmony with the need.

Finally the Lord is presented as "the beginning of the creation of God" (3:14). This statement does not mean that Jesus Christ is the first of all created beings, and therefore He Himself is a created being. Such an interpretation would conflict with all that the Word of God teaches about Him. We have noted the reference to Laodicea in Paul's Epistle to the Colossians. Apparently the two churches, being in close geographical proximity to each other, had been afflicted with the same error. Both had robbed Christ of His essential deity, thereby making Him less than God. Those persons who tell us that Jesus was the first person to be created by God are in error.

What did our Lord mean when He said He is "the beginning of the creation of God"? We must never depart from the fundamental principle of Biblical interpretation that each Scripture must be understood in the light of all Scripture. Paul described this principle in the phrase, "comparing spiritual things with spiritual" (1 Corinthians 2:13). Now when we examine Paul's statement to the Colossians, which he instructed to be read in the church at Laodicea, we have divine light on our Lord's description of Himself in Revelation 3:14.

Paul presented Christ as "the image of the invisible God, the firstborn of every creature" (Colossians 1:15). The apostle is not saying that Jesus is the first person to be created. Christ is connected with creation, but only as the Creator. Paul continues, "For by Him were all things created, that are in heaven, and that are in earth, visible and invisible, whether they be thrones, or dominions, or principalities, or powers: all things were created by Him, and for Him: And He is before all things, and by Him all things consist'' (Colossians 1:16-17). John begins his Gospel record by saying, ''All things were made by Him; and without Him was not any thing made that was made'' (John 1:3). Jesus, John, and Paul are all saying the same thing. Christ commenced the process of creation after He had initiated the plan of creation. He was the originator of all creation, the first cause of all created things. Everything that the human eye has ever seen, whether on earth or in the heavens, and all that remains for man to see, is the work of Christ. All creation testifies of Him.

Three significant creations are mentioned in the Bible:

First, there is the *natural* creation over which God placed Adam as its head. But Adam and his posterity failed. The dispensation of the *natural* creation under Adam ended in disaster and divine judgment. The human family continued in its course of apostasy away from God.

Secondly, there is the *national* creation over which God placed Abraham as its father. From the loins of Abraham there arose the nation of Israel. No nation among all the nations on earth has been endowed with privileges equal to those God gave to Abraham and his posterity. But Israel failed God and the *national* creation ended in judgment upon God's chosen people.

Thirdly, there is the *new* creation. In this dispensation of grace, which has now continued for more than nineteen centuries, we are witnessing more plainly than ever the corruption in the human heart. The new creation in the present dispensation is the Church. Paul wrote,

"Therefore if any man be in Christ, he is a new creature [creation]" (2 Corinthians 5:17). Like every other instrument before it, the church has failed in her witness for God. As we have seen in the present series of studies, the Christian profession becomes increasingly inferior until, when Christ returns, it is utterly rejected. The failure is due to the church's refusal to acknowledge the Lord Jesus Christ as the sovereign Head of the church and to follow the truth. In view of this growing apostasy our Lord presents Himself as "the Amen, the faithful and true witness, the beginning of the creation of God."

The Delusion the Church Suffered

The one great peril threatening the church at Laodicea was the false opinion of itself. Unitedly its members said, "I am rich, and increased with goods, and have need of nothing" (Revelation 3:17). Here is the language of complacency, smugness, independence, self-satisfaction. Before John penned the Revelation he wrote in an earlier Epistle, "If we say that we have no sin, we deceive ourselves, and the truth is not in us" (1 John 1:8). In Laodicea the church members could see no fault in themselves. They were saying, "We have no sin," but they were deceiving themselves. They were deluded. They were guilty of the very sin against which the Christian is warned. Paul wrote, "For I say, through the grace given unto me, to every man that is among you, not to think of himself more highly than he ought to think; but to think soberly, according as God hath dealt to every man the measure of faith" (Romans 12:3).

The beginning of all true success is to see ourselves as we are. The Laodiceans said, "I am rich, and increased with goods, and have need of nothing." Christ said, "Thou art wretched, and miserable, and poor, and blind, and naked." They were so self-opinionated as to be deluded and deceived as to their true condition. This condition marks the greatest tragedy in the history of Christendom. The professing church, which is one day to be repudiated by the Lord, is unconscious of her miserable condition, ignorant of the terrible threat hanging over her, and blind to the truth which had been given her. Such is the deplorable state of the church in the last days before Christ comes. The things of the world and of the flesh have taken the place of Christ and the written Word of God.

Many pastors and their church officers delight to show me their new buildings, and they usually mention how much money those buildings cost. They have boasted of the growing staff and annual budget. They seem to have whatever they want. Ninety out of one hundred churches see no need of a time for confession, humiliation, and prayer. They are well attended on Sunday morning but there is no apparent need for the deepening of spiritual life. They are satisfied with things as they are. The need of the Headship of Christ and the power of the Holy Spirit seem to be unknown. The churches are rich in number, rich in organization, rich in material wealth, rich in academic learning, and rich in an army of paid workers, but they are like Samson who "wist not that the LORD was departed from him" (Judges 16:20).

If you were to start out on a tour of churches in America to learn about their spiritual condition, I would warn you to brace yourself for a shock. You will find Bible-carrying church members who are unspiritual, if not unsaved. You will find a preponderance of churchgoers who are involved in a variety of worldly activities such as illicit sex, alcoholism, dishonest business deals, and the like. You will find in some instances these people holding positions of leadership and authority. They plan the church's programs, manage the finances, hire and fire pastors, yet they are ignorant of God's Word, know nothing of the leading of the Holy Spirit, and refuse to submit themselves to the Headship of the Lord Jesus Christ.

We are in the Laodicean stage of church history, the last days before the return of our Lord. We are witnessing the rise of the "people's church" where the "people's rights" prevail. They form quite a high opinion of themselves and thus they have need of nothing. But they are duped, deluded, deceived. As we shall see at the close of this present study, professing Christianity will be ultimately rejected by our Lord when He returns. He said, "I will spue thee out of My mouth." When He comes, conditions upon this earth will be as godless and as vile as those in the antedeluvian world, for, "as the days of Noah were, so shall also the coming of the Son of man be" (Matthew 24:37).

The Diagnosis Christ Saw

Jesus said, "I know thy works, that thou art neither cold nor hot: I would thou wert cold or hot. So then because thou art lukewarm, and neither cold nor hot, I will spue thee out of My mouth" (Revelation 3:15-16). The prognostication of the Laodicean church begins with a picture of almost plain crudeness. The church had been infected with a nauseating quality which will make Christ vomit them out of His mouth. They were neither cold to the point of freezing nor hot to the boiling point. In spiritual matters they were halfhearted, nominally Christian, tastelessly tepid, enough to make the stomach turn. That is the way the church at Laodicea affected the Lord. It is an unpleasant sight, nevertheless true. He does not see total frigid indifference nor does He see fervent heat, only lukewarm indifference. It was a condition utterly repugnant to Christ.

The figure our Lord employed to describe the condition of the church in Laodicea is a solemn one. It is the figure of a drink of water. A hot drink is palatable and refreshing in its effect. A cold drink is likewise refreshing. Jesus said to His disciples, ''And whosoever shall give to drink unto one of these little ones a cup of cold water only in the name of a disciple, verily I say unto you, he shall in no wise lose his reward'' (Matthew 10:42). Why did He say *cold* water? Lukewarm water is an emetic. It is unpleasant to him who swallows it. It has a nauseating, sickening effect, turning the stomach. It is this figure the Lord used to describe the condition of the church at Laodicea. He is saying, ''Your spiritual condition is nauseating to me. You make me sick to my stomach. I am about to spue you out of my mouth.'' When Christ comes again He will not tolerate her any longer but will reject her in disgust.

Next, the Lord rebuked the church for its emphasis on material wealth. The church said, ''I am rich, and increased with goods, and have need of nothing.'' Jesus said, "Thou art wretched, and miserable, and poor, and blind, and naked" (3:17). What self-deception! They were boasting of their material prosperity but spiritually they were beggarly-poor, poverty-stricken. The Lord's diagnosis is not flattering.

He said the church was "wretched." This word appears one other time in the New Testament where Paul said of himself, "O wretched man that I am" (Romans 7:24). The word "wretched" means "distressed." When Paul saw Himself as God saw him, he was a distressed person groaning under the burden of indwelling sin and longing for deliverance. Of course, the term is used here by Christ to refer to the spiritual condition of the church at Laodicea. The difference between Paul and the Laodiceans is clear. Paul recognized his wretchedness; the Laodiceans did not, thus they were blinded by their own self-deception. They thought they were doing well in their religious life but they were in great distress and not aware of it. The Word of God says, "If a man think himself to be something, when he is nothing, he deceiveth himself" (Galatians 6:3).

Christ then describes that church as being "miserable." The Greek word means "pitiable, or to be pitied." Paul used the same word when he wrote, "If in this life only we have hope in Christ, we are of all men most miserable [to be pitied]" (1 Corinthians 15:19). I'm certain in my own mind that there were Christians who were not in the church at Laodicea who envied those who were in, but the Lord looked upon them with pity. He actually felt sorry for them.

He described them further as being "poor." Here again

we see the tragedy of Laodicea, namely, they were proud of their wealth and blind to their poverty. Judged by human standards they had the richest church in town, but the risen Lord declared them to be poverty-stricken. They didn't have a thing that was worth having. Our Lord said to the covetous Pharisees, "That which is highly esteemed among men is abomination in the sight of God" (Luke 16:15). Never before in all her long history has the visible church had such a large membership; never before has she owned as much property; never before has she spent so much money on buildings and payroll. Yet the Lord affirms that she is poor. Material wealth and spiritual poverty often accompany one another. There is a wealth that is poverty.

The Lord said the Laodiceans were "blind." They lacked vision. They could see neither their spiritual poverty nor their plight. The church that does not see her spiritual poverty and her need of God is blind. Actually there was the lack of spiritual discernment, a condition characteristic of all who have not been born again. "The natural man receiveth not the things of the Spirit of God: for they are foolishness unto him: neither can he know them, because they are spiritually discerned" (1 Corinthians 2:14).

Finally, Christ said that the church was "naked." Laodicea was famous for the garments manufactured there and shipped to the known world. Their woolen garments were a luxury item sought by men and women everywhere. But while they prided themselves on the garments they produced, they were spiritually naked. A person may appear wearing the most exquisite and costly garments this world can produce and the soul have no covering but the filthy rags of self-righteousness. Such was our Lord's diagnosis of the church at Laodicea.

The Direction Christ Submitted

Our Lord has some words of counsel for this church. He knows that there are some of His own in the assembly at Laodicea, so He submits a course for them to follow. He knows that some of those who are saved will see the error of their ways, admit that they were wrong and repent. They will be a small minority, among the twenty-five per cent represented by the good soil in the parable of the sower, the children of the kingdom in the parable of the wheat and the tares. Some will be saved Jews and others saved Gentiles, as indicated in the parable of the pearl of great price, the good fish in the parable of the net and the fishes. To them He says, "As many as I love, I rebuke and chasten: be zealous therefore, and repent" (Revelation 3:19).

I never cease to marvel at the love and patience and compassion God shows toward His children. He has a way all His own of bringing us to see where we are wrong and how we should amend our conduct. The Lord Jesus expressed it when He said, "I love, I rebuke and chasten." It is the idea of divine discipline and it runs through the entire Bible. As a matter of fact, Christ was quoting from a proverb which says, "My son, despise not the chastening of the LORD; neither be weary of His correction: For whom the Lord loveth He correcteth; even as a father the son in whom he delighteth" (Proverbs 3:11-12). Lest we forget, there is a reminder in the New Testament which says, "And ye have forgotten the exhortation which speaketh unto you as unto children, My son, despise not thou the chastening of the Lord, nor faint when thou art rebuked of Him: For whom the Lord loveth He chasteneth, and scourgeth every son whom He receiveth. If ye endure chastening, God dealeth with you as with sons; for what son is he whom the father chasteneth not?" (Hebrews 12:5-7) Those who are truly born again have a heavenly Father who, in love and with compassion, corrects them. "Blessed is the man whom Thou chastenest, O LORD, and teachest him out of Thy law" (Psalm 94:12). "Behold, happy is the man whom God correcteth: therefore despise not thou the chastening of the Almighty" (Job 5:17). "But when we are judged, we are chastened of the Lord, that we should not be condemned with the world" (1 Corinthians 11:32).

The Lord now submits to the church a course to follow. He says, "I counsel thee to buy of Me gold tried in the fire, that thou mayest be rich; and white raiment, that thou mayest be clothed, and that the shame of thy nakedness do not appear; and anoint thine eyes with eyesalve, that thou mayest see" (Revelation 3:18). He is not telling them that salvation can be purchased with gold. Money is not the coin of the realm in Christ's kingdom. The sinner cannot purchase redemption with silver or gold (1 Peter 1:18-19). In the parables of the treasure and the pearl, Christ sold all that He had and purchased the field (Matthew 13:44-46). Laodicea prided itself in its wealth, so as long as they imagine they are rich they will not buy gold. A person who has everything he needs and wants will not buy anything. What Christ is trying to do here is to impress upon them the idea that they do have a need, that they are lacking in the things they need and do not have.

The gold and white raiment and eyesalve are figures of speech that the Laodiceans could understand. They were a wealthy people. Their city manufactured and exported the finest quality clothing and a famous eyesalve for diseases of the eye. These products were exported to every part of the civilized world. But the people did not possess Christ's true riches, "the riches of His grace" (Ephesians 1:7), "the riches of His goodness" (Romans 2:4), nor "the riches of His glory" (Romans 9:23). So they must receive Him who alone possesses what they need.

But what did Christ mean when He counseled them to buy these things? I see a bit of irony in the seeming contradiction in our Lord's words. But we know of course that there is no contradiction. He was offering them His righteousness, His wisdom, and these are available for the taking. True wealth, true garments, true wisdom, and true perception are in Christ Himself. Now, He is not for sale. The Prophet Isaiah wrote, "Ho, every one that thirsteth, come ye to the waters, and he that hath no money; come ye, buy, and eat; yea, come, buy wine and milk without money and without price" (Isaiah 55:1). Yes, it is all available without money and without price. The counsel Christ gives is to individuals in the church. "He that hath an ear, let him hear what the Spirit saith unto the church-es" (Revelation 3:22). In the most miserable church there are still some individuals who are Christ's true people. To all such He submits a course to follow: "Be zealous therefore, and repent'' (3:19).

The pronouncement of judgment is upon the professing church as a whole, and it is unconditional and absolute. The judgment upon Christendom is inevitable. What will the churches be like when our Lord comes? There is an intentional arrangement in the order of the seven letters. Laodicea represents the final period in church history. The Laodicean church is the church of the end times, and it is not good.

The rejection of Laodicea synchronizes prophetically in time with the removal of Philadelphia. Philadelphia is *caught up* to be with the Lord, while Laodicea is *cast out*. The last two phases of Christian profession are both viewed in our Lord's last parable in the series of the seven parables in Matthew 13. The good fish are gathered but the bad are cast away (Matthew 13:48).

Dear reader, be warned in time. God will not allow His house in Heaven to be degraded by the presence of sinful and godless people who have rejected His Son. ''Believe on the Lord Jesus Christ, and thou shalt be saved.''

CONCLUSION

CHRIST KNOCKING AT THE DOOR

Behold, I stand at the door, and knock: if any man hear My voice, and open the door, I will come in to him, and will sup with him, and he with Me (Revelation 3:20).

Here is a most touching picture revealing our Lord's tenderness and compassion. He had just said, "I counsel thee" (3:18). He might have commanded and compelled, but instead He invited and entreated. But His counsel had been rejected. Nineteen hundred years of church history proves that His offer has been slighted and spurned, His entreaty has met only with contempt and scorn. And so, before He finally spues forth the professing church, He takes up His position outside its door. What wonderful grace is here shown! What marvelous condescension to knock upon the very door of the church which, though calling itself by His name, has no place for Him inside. He is not exercising His divine prerogatives nor asserting His supreme authority. The day of grace has not yet run its course.

Of the many artists' conceptions of Christ that have been painted during the centuries, none has appeared more frequently than the one of Him standing outside the door and knocking. Before I attempt to explain verse 20, I will tell you that this verse is not an appeal to the unsaved, but rather a call to the saved. I find no Scripture in support of the popular idea that Christ is knocking at the sinner's heart, and that in order to receive the Saviour he must open the door of his heart and allow Christ to come in. There is no door the sinner must open to receive salvation. Jesus said, ''I am the door: by Me if any man enter in, he shall be saved, and shall go in and out, and find pasture'' (John 10:9). If the closing chapter of this book should meet the eye of anyone who has not been born again, remember that Christ the Door stands wide open before you. It is not merely ''ajar'' as the hymn writer put it, but it is wide open, and all you must do is to walk in. Our Lord said, ''Him that cometh to Me I will in no wise cast out'' (John 6:37).

The words of Christ, ''Behold, I stand at the door, and knock: if any man hear My voice, and open the door, I will come in to him, and will sup with him, and he with Me,'' is not an appeal to the sinner but to the saint. The central thought in these words is not the sinner's *union* with Christ but the saint's *communion* with Him. And don't miss the important fact that the call is essentially an individual one.

Inside many churches today there is little or no communion with the Lord Jesus Christ. For the most part, the congregations in churches are not gathered in His name to worship Him. Christendom has cast Him out. The modern church congregation is being entertained with religious activities which cater to the flesh. They speak and sing about *Jesus*, but not the Jesus of the Bible. It is ''another Jesus'' (2 Corinthians 11:4), that is, another of a different kind.

The Christ of the Bible is the excluded Christ, excluded

from the church for which He died. He put His Church in the world to let her light shine, but the world got into the church and cast Him out. Christendom has no place for Him. Modern churches are feasting upon the things which the world supplies. They have no desire to sup with Christ, hence the door remains closed against Him. The Laodicean church of these last days has everything in it except the Lord Jesus Christ.

Christ is excluded from His world. Were He to appear in Person before the United Nations, world leaders would not admit Him. Were He to come to Israel and Egypt and offer them His peace program, they would turn Him away. Were He to present Himself to the president and congress of the United States, would He be welcome? But one day the position will be reversed. The very ones who cast Him out will be facing the closed door. That day is pictured vividly in our Lord's parable of the ten virgins. ''The bridegroom came; and they that were ready went in with Him to the marriage: and *the door was shut*. Afterward came also the other virgins, saying, Lord, Lord, open to us. But He answered and said, Verily I say unto you, I know you not'' (Matthew 25:10-12).

One day, possibly soon, the Laodicean church will be knocking at the door, but then it will be too late. Christ will have gathered His true Church unto Himself. Many in Christendom shall call to Him but no voice will answer; they will seek Him but they will not find Him. The day of grace will have run its course.

There are some solemn words in the book of Proverbs which apply here. Read them slowly and attentively, ponder them seriously: ''Because I have called, and ye refused; I have stretched out My hand, and no man regarded; But ye have set at nought all My counsel, and would none of My reproof: I also will laugh at your calamity; I will mock when your fear cometh; When your fear cometh as desolation, and your destruction cometh as a whirlwind; when distress and anguish cometh upon you. Then shall they call upon Me, but I will not answer; they shall seek Me early, but they shall not find Me: For that they hated knowledge, and did not choose the fear of the LORD: They would none of My counsel: they despised all My reproof; Therefore shall they eat of the fruit of their own way, and be filled with their own devices'' (Proverbs 1:24-31).

Our Lord's appeal in Revelation 3:20 is to the individual. It is the individual believer who must open the door, and when he does, a blessed feast and fellowship await him. ''If any man hear My voice, and open the door, I will come in to him, and will sup with him, and he with Me.'' I am personally convinced that we are in the last days of the Laodicean period in church history. Fellow believers, the Lord is now standing and knocking, seeking the place He deserves in the hearts of His own. If we will surrender to Him the place which is His, He will feed us with His riches and fill us with joy and peace. Mary supped with the Lord when she ''sat at Jesus' feet, and heard His Word'' (Luke 10:39). Let us not be satisfied until we are supping with the Lord Himself.

Yes, the Lord is knocking and waiting. He is not waiting for the World Council of Churches to admit Him. He is not waiting for the National Council of Churches to open their door to Him. He is not waiting for a committee in your local church to pass a resolution to make Him the Head of that church. He waits for a man, a woman, a young person, any person who will allow Him to enter and take command. He is waiting for you and me who, surrounded by an abundance of material things, will say, "I am convinced of my wretchedness, my poverty, my blindness and nakedness. Come Lord Jesus and take control. I need Thee."

Now I must warn you that any Christian in this Laodicean age who should open the door to a day-by-day intimate communion with the Lord Jesus Christ might find himself excluded from the average church. When Mary sat at Jesus' feet to commune with Him she was not popular with her sister Martha. Yet Jesus Himself testified that Mary had chosen that good part (Luke 10:42). Fellowship with Christ means a new standard of life, a new set of principles to govern day by day behavior, a new love for the Word of God and a desire to study it, a new concern and compassion for lost sinners. This is the fruit of fellowship with Christ, and it is not present in the Laodicean church.

One day Jesus healed a blind man. The man insisted upon being loyal to Christ. When the religious leaders witnessed the man's unswerving dedication to the Lord, they excommunicated him from the synagogue. When Jesus knew what had happened, He found the man and gave him reassurance. The man responded with the words, "Lord, I believe." Then John added the words, "And he worshipped Him" (John 9:38). The man who opened the door to communion with Christ was cast out of the place of public worship, but he enjoyed sweet communion with the One who alone makes possible true worship.

Dr. G. Campbell Morgan said, "It may be that the Laodicean church will exclude the man who includes Christ. Then let that man have no sorrow in his heart save for the folly of the church. If there be no other way to find Christ than by leaving the Laodicean church, then the sooner it be left, the better." In these days when conflicting religious voices are heard like a Babel speaking in so many different tongues, the corporate recovery of Christendom is hopeless. The large denominations refuse to heed the appeal of the risen Christ. So let us as individual Christians give heed to Christ's call.

In the letters to the seven churches, we have seen seven types of congregations. Since congregations are made up of people, it is not incorrect to conclude that here we find seven different kinds of Christians, any or all of which can be found in any one congregation. When you have a church where one type prevails, that assembly may be designated as that type. It is true of both individual Christians as well as individual churches that all seven types have appeared during the entire Christian dispensation. But, as has been pointed out in our study, the seven types of churches present a prophetic unfolding of the spiritual condition of the church in seven successive stages of her history. The Laodicean church represents the period of growing apostasy from the start of the twentieth century until Christ returns to earth in judgment. The apostasy reaches its worst in the Laodicean church.

In conclusion let us consider the central correspondence between the seventh parable in Matthew 13 and this seventh epistle. In the seventh parable the kingdom of heaven, which is Christendom or the Christian profession, is likened unto a net which gathered every kind of fish. The net is drawn to shore and a process of separation begins. The good fish are gathered into vessels and the bad are cast away.

In the Laodicean church, the visible church today, the net is filled with every kind of fish. Never before has there been such a conglomerate variety as there now is in the professed church of Christ. Almost every shade of political opinion and religion congregate on a common platform under the name of Christianity. One might see atheists, materialists, rationalists, ritualists, pantheists, spiritists, moralists, theosophists, and homosexuals finding both accommodation and a hearing in the circles of nominal Christians. Whether we like it or not, the Laodicean letter presents an accurate picture of conditions in Christendom today.

But the scene is not totally bad. More and more the real Christians are withdrawing themselves from various systems and gathering in churches and assemblies for the study of God's Word and the spreading of the gospel of Christ. These are the good fish in our Lord's seventh parable, the Philadelphian type with an open door of opportunity for evangelism.

When our Lord returns He will gather the good fish to Himself, but the bad will be cast forth or spued out by Him, to be judged for their rejection of Him. The dominant truth in both parable and epistle is *judgment*. The Laodicean state of the professing church is the final one. There is no eighth epistle.

Every prophetic forecast as presented in the seven

church epistles, save two, has now become history. They have been literally and actually fulfilled. The only remaining events are the removal of the Philadelphian saints and the utter rejection of the Laodicean shams. Be warned in time, you who have despised God's mercy. Trust in the Lord Jesus Christ and God will save you.

BIBLIOGRAPHY

Arnot, W. *The Parables of Our Lord.* New York: Nelson, 1884.

Ayer, William Ward. *Christ's Parables for Today.* New Jersey: Revell, 1949.

Barclay, William. *The Gospel of Matthew.* Philadelphia, Pennsylvania: Westminster, 1959.

_____. *The Revelation of John.* Philadelphia, Pennsylvania: Westminster, 1961.

Barker, C.L. *The Revelation.* New York: Carlton Press, 1964.

Brooks, Frederick L. *The Key to God's Program.* Chattanooga, Tennessee: Author, 1937.

Bruce, Alexander B. *The Parabolic Teaching of Christ.* New York: A.C. Armstrong, 1908.

Cooper, David L. *Future Events Foretold.* Los Angeles, California: Author, 1935.

Criswell, W.A. *Expository Sermons on Revelation.* Michigan: Zondervan, 1964.

English, E.S. *Studies in the Gospel According to Matthew.* New York: Revell, 1935.

Fereday, W.W. *Our Lord's Miracles and Parables.* Kilmarnock, 1866.

Fraser, A. *The First Four Parables of the Kingdom of Heaven.* Scottsdale, Pennsylvania: Evangelical Fellowship, 1954.

Gaebelein, A.C. *The Gospel of Matthew.* Neptune, New Jersey: Loizeaux Brothers, 1961.

Harris, W. *Miracles and Parables of the Old Testament.* Grand Rapids, Michigan: Baker Book House, 1959.

Havner, Vance. *Repent or Else.* New Jersey: Revell, 1958.

Hoeksema, Herman. *Behold He Cometh.* Grand Rapids, Michigan: Kregel Publications, 1969.

Hoyt, Herman A. *Studies in Revelation.* Indiana: BMH Books, 1977.

Ironside, H.A. *Notes on Matthew.* Neptune, New Jersey: Loizeaux Brothers, 1948.

Kelly, William. *Lectures on Matthew.* New York: Loizeaux Brothers, 1948.

Lang, G.H. *The Parabolic Teaching of Scripture.* Grand Rapids, Michigan: Eerdmans, 1955.

Larkin, Clarence. *The Book of Revelation.* Philadelphia, Pennsylvania: Larkin Estate, 1919.

Lockyer, Herbert. *All the Parables of the Bible.* Grand Rapids, Michigan: Zondervan, 1963.

Morgan, G. Campbell. *The Gospel According to Matthew.* New Jersey: Revell, 1929.

_____. *The Parables and Metaphors of Our Lord.* New Jersey: Revell, 1929.

Mounce, Robert H. *The Book of Revelation.* Grand Rapids, Michigan: Eerdmans, 1977.

Newell, William R. *The Book of Revelation.* Chicago, Illinois: Moody Press, 1935.

Palmer, E.W. *The Key to the Bible.* Chicago, 1957.

Pink, Arthur W. *The Parables of Matthew Thirteen.* Covington, Kentucky, 1961.

Plummer, Alfred. *An Exegetical Commentary on the Gospel According to Matthew.* Grand Rapids, Michigan: Eerdmans, 1953.

Ryle, J.C. *Expository Thoughts on the Gospels.* Greenwood, South Carolina: Attic Press, 1856.

Ryrie, Charles C. *Revelation.* Chicago, Illinois: Moody Press, 1966.

Walvoord, John F. *Matthew—Thy Kindom Come.* Chicago, Illinois: Moody Press, 1974.

_____. *The Revelation of Jesus Christ.* Chicago, Illinois: Moody Press, 1966.

INDEX OF SCRIPTURE TEXTS